The Old Paths
of Gloucestershire

The Old Paths
of Gloucestershire

Alan Pilbeam

First published in 2008 by Tempus Publishing

Reprinted in 2011 by
The History Press
The Mill, Brimscombe Port,
Stroud, Gloucestershire, GL5 2QG
www.thehistorypress.co.uk

Reprinted 2013

British Library Cataloguing in Publication Data.
A catalogue record for this book is available from the British Library.

ISBN 978 0 7524 4540 3

Typesetting and origination by
The History Press
Printed and bound in Great Britain

Contents

Introduction

Even a cursory glance at a large-scale Ordnance Survey map is sufficient to remind the map reader of the numerous paths and tracks that cross the countryside. The red or green, dotted or dashed lines that symbolise the paths, produce a network pattern that with varying density covers the whole map. In Gloucestershire there are over 2,500 miles of public footpaths and about 220 miles of bridleways, as well as other unmetalled roads. Most of the tarmac roads, including the main roads, first came into existence as footpaths. The questions – when was a particular footpath formed? why was it there? who used it? what did the travellers see along the route? – are often difficult, and sometimes impossible, to answer, but they are still worth asking. The search for answers to these questions may lead to new insights into life long ago and to a greater appreciation of the making of the landscape, for it has been rightly said that footpaths are 'one of man's oldest inscriptions on the landscape'.

Until the mid-nineteenth century footpaths were mainly used by local people, and it was rare for the latter to travel for more than a day's walk from home. Indeed, there had been old laws preventing travel for greater distances. From 1388 letters of passage were required by people wishing to go further. So pilgrims, messengers, pedlars, and in later years drovers, all required a licence for more distant journeys. Such legislation kept people to their own or neighbouring parishes, and stabilised the population. And in addition to the legal restraints on travel, it was often dangerous to walk outside the home territory. Those that did so were viewed with suspicion, as most likely to be beggars, homeless paupers or thieves.

Travelling on foot was generally out of necessity rather than from choice. The gentry were usually transported by carriage, even over the short distances from their homes to church. Walking was the mode of travel of the common people, in fact the word travel is derived from travail and implies suffering and labour.

Some leisure walking by the middle and upper classes had begun in the last two decades of the eighteenth century and the first decades of the nineteenth century. By then many roads had been improved by turnpiking, land enclosure had fixed the paths, and the countryside was safer from footpads. But the paths taken by these walking tourists were chosen for their destinations, rather than for the interest of the routes. Sites of antiquity, picturesque views that could be sketched and spectacular natural phenomena such as waterfalls, cliffs and exposed rocks, were sought out. The actual paths to them were relatively unimportant. The Romantic poets and artists stimulated this type of interest, and the early guidebooks, written to assist the tourist, emphasised that the chief benefit of walking was in reaching the destination! In this way the leisure walker was following the practice of the medieval pilgrim seeking out a shrine and the eighteenth-century drover going to the fair.

Belas Knap. A restored Neolithic long barrow. Notice the dry-stone walling of the western horn of the barrow and the dry-stone wall behind, with the unfortunate use of more durable York stone in the stile.

A view north from Symonds Yat, one of the most famous viewpoints overlooking the Wye Valley.

The Buck Stone, near Staunton. A massive boulder of Quartz Conglomerate, which was once a rocking stone perched on one of the highest points of the Forest of Dean.

However, by the end of the nineteenth century, it had become widely recognised that the best way to become familiar with an area was to walk its footpaths. As long ago as 1879, Richard Jefferies wrote 'they only know a country who are acquainted with its footpaths'. In 1887 Thomas Hardy walked in the south west of England in order to better prepare himself for writing *Tess of the D'Urbervilles*. In the early twentieth century regional geographers began to walk their specialist areas, and in the 1950s the geographer S.W. Wooldridge recommended learning through the sole of the foot and the historian W.G. Hoskins noted that 'the variety and detail of the landscape that pleases the eye and the mind is only observed as one travels on foot and unhurriedly'. So walking for its value as a form of physical exercise and for the interest of the path itself, with its trees and flowers, its birds and insects, its scents and sounds, its geology and scenery, and its varied weather, came a century later than the first leisure walking. Nowadays, when paths have clear waymarking, well-maintained stiles and gates, and when there is strong legislation for path protection, this is the most popular use of footpaths.

To increase our enjoyment as we walk these paths today, it is helpful to remember those who have travelled that way before, to try to appreci-

An attractive footpath through flowery grassland along the slopes of the Coln Valley near Withington.

ate something of their thoughts and aspirations, and to note the things that they saw. This is not an easy task, for although the paths were first marked out by human feet and have been compared to veins for the circulation of human life, the centuries-long continuity of traditional rural life and landscape has been broken by a powerful set of modern factors. First came the eighteenth-century Enclosure Movement that often destroyed a sense of place by removing so many traditional landscape features. Then the late nineteenth-century acquisition of land by 'new money' diminished the influence on the countryside and its use of the old landed gentry. Much more recently, the combination of intensive farming methods, rapid rural population turnover, changing attitudes to wildlife and its conservation, greater urban mobility though widespread car ownership, and the increased wealth and technology of the people who use the countryside, have largely severed the links between past and present users of footpaths. This book is designed to restore an understanding of those links, to renew the connections, and so to contribute to the modern walker's appreciation and enjoyment.

The general developments in the history of footpaths and their uses are here applied to the paths and tracks of Gloucestershire. Most of our paths were originally made for parish use, for villagers journeying to work in the fields and woods, or to church, market and mill, and they probably go back in time to the origins of the rural settlements themselves. Nearly all of Gloucestershire's rural settlements are recorded in the Domesday Book of 1086, so it is likely that many paths were in existence by then. The case study of the parishes in the upper Windrush valley in chapter eleven illustrates this. Similarly, the paths radiating from eighteenth- and nineteenth-century mines and mills, considered in chapter six, were for miners and weavers in their journeys to and from work. For six days a week these paths were used by labourers, but on the Sunday, when most work ceased, they were used for casual wandering, as villagers walked the fields and woods with a freedom hard rural toil did not otherwise allow. There were, however, other paths that from medieval times onwards were followed by long-distance travellers such as the pilgrims who visited the four shrines in the county, the drovers taking Welsh cattle to the fairs supplying London's meat market, and the bow hauliers working along the river and canal towpaths. We discuss these paths and their visible features in chapters two, four and five. The devastations of the English Civil War, as soldiers of both King and Parliament roamed the country between engagements in battle, were associated with the strategically chosen paths followed in chapter three. The Cheltenham promenades, considered in chapter seven, were laid out, at least in part, to display the elegant clothes of those 'taking the waters', and likewise the garden paths of chapter eight disclosed exotic flowers and plants and fashionable landscaping designs. Chapter nine retraces some early leisure paths in the Forest of Dean and chapter ten explores a modern counterpart along the Cotswold edge. But we will begin with some paths that had to be followed with great precision because they had the important function of marking out land boundaries.

ONE

Perambulations

When land transactions took place in the years before the skills of drawing accurate plans had been developed, the area of land to be given, exchanged or sold, was defined by a perambulation. This was a detailed description of a walk around the boundary of the piece of land, in which the key visible features along the route were listed. In the Saxon period such perambulations were recorded as land charters. For about twenty-five different places in Gloucestershire, Saxon land charters or copies of the original charters have survived.

Boundary landmarks recorded in the charters such as buildings, isolated trees, boundary stones and many ancient monuments have long since disappeared from the landscape, but the boundaries that followed such features as ancient paths and trackways may still be identified and in some cases these correspond to present day parish boundaries. The boundary landmarks that were physical features such as hills, valleys and springs remain virtually unchanged, and the place names associated with these features are important in determining the boundary because, as the place-name scholar Margaret Gelling has shown, there was a greater degree of precision in Saxon place names than is commonly appreciated. Thus rather than indicating general types of terrain, the Saxon references were quite specific. A 'cumbe', now the place name suffix –combe, was a short steep sided valley, a 'dene' was a long tapering valley, and a 'dune', now usually spelt 'down', was a low rounded hill about 200ft above the surrounding land.

Sometimes a Saxon charter boundary has been preserved in the present-day landscape by a hedgerow, and such a hedge will be distinguished from others in the area by the wide range of shrubs growing in it. Old hedgerows on the Cotswolds and in the Vale of Gloucester are those which include not only the hawthorn and blackthorn shrubs that were planted because they are stock proof, but also hazel, spindle, dogwood, oak, field maple, crab apple, ash and similar species that have naturally colonised the hedge after their seeds were brought to it by birds or the wind. Often these hedges are also parish boundaries and they may date back to the times of the charters or earlier. So observations in the field, careful interpretation of place names, and the interpolation of unknown boundary markers from those that can be identified, may all help in following a Saxon charter perambulation.

A well-known example of a Saxon charter in which the perambulation is for 'feld' relates to land at Hawling, high on the Cotswolds midway between Cheltenham and Stow-on-the-Wold. It was originally thought that the charter dated from about AD 980 but it is now considered to be a little later. It refers to a block of land which was granted to the Abbey of Worcester at this time. The possible route of the perambulation was traced in the field by the historian H.P.R. Finberg, and although some of his suggestions have been subsequently criticised, his investigation is

The parish church and lych gate at Hawling.

an interesting example of the type of research involved in attempting to follow an old charter boundary. The charter, with a rough translation, together with Finberg's suggested OS grid references and comments on the reasons for selecting the specific locations, are set out below:

Aerest aet thaes Bernes Ende aet thaes Waeteres Sprynge – beginning at the barn's end by the water spring [073228]. Possibly the barn would have been at a distance from the village and used as a base for farming activity there. We would not expect the building to have lasted for 1,000 years but the spring should be identifiable, and the grid reference above is to the most powerful spring in the whole parish, where a hydraulic ram has been used to pump water to higher ground. An alternative suggested site is to one of the springs on the north side of the village, for example at 065231, and this assumes that the barn was close to the farmsteads and other farm buildings in the village.

Aefter tham Waetere into Hallinga Homme – from the spring to Hawling ham [081234].

For the Hawling ham, which may be a 'piece of valley bottom land hemmed in by higher ground', there is at this grid reference near

The *grenan weg* of the Saxon charter, now a bridleway following the Hawling parish boundary.

A junction of paths near the Tally Ho, several of which are more than 1,000 years old. The signpost marks one of the turning points of the perambulation.

Hawling Lodge, a small triangular area of land, flat and beside a stream. Valleys from both spring sites converge here.

Of Hallinga Homme into Rames Cumbe – from Hawling ham to the rams' combe [085234].

Rams would have been kept in a walled or fenced enclosure and its site could only be guessed at, but a suitably shaped valley corresponding to the place name 'combe' is found here.

Aefter tham Grenan Wege into thaere Mylnstige - along the green way to the up hill mill path [091232]. Green ways are old tracks which were often used for moving livestock and the bridle way which follows the Hawling parish boundary here is just such a track, and it leads to the only possible site for an early water mill in the parish. There is no trace of a water mill today, which is surprising as mill sites were usually continuously occupied. Perhaps there was insufficient water for successful mill operations. We may note, however, that an ornamental pond has been dug here recently. The combination of parish boundary and bridle way is significant.

Of ... into Cylesdene to theam Haran Stane – from the mill into Cyle's dean to the hoar stone [083221]. The mill path goes into a long gently sloping valley, a 'dene', which is followed by the parish boundary. The valley is now wooded, but woods come and go quite frequently in the history of a landscape. Where a boundary sharply changed direction a stone was placed to act as a marker. This possibly occurred here where the present parish boundary makes a right-angle bend, and similarly with the next marker. Probably both Cyle and Scobbe are personal names.

Of ... into Scobbe Stane – on to Scobbe's stone [083220].

Of ... suth to tham Lytlan Beorge – south to the little barrow, or tumulus. There is no field or documentary evidence of a tumulus in this area.

Ond swa suth ofer Turcendene into tham Crum Daele – and south over Turkdean to the quarry [063207]. Old quarries are numerous in this part of the Cotswolds and so are not very helpful for identifying charter boundaries but the neighbouring village of Turkdean lies at the lower end of another long valley which slopes gently to the south east. The perambulation crossed this valley and this fact helps in locating a possible old quarry site. It lies beside an old road and such a location would have made it easier for the transport of stone.

Of ... suth ond west to thaere Ealdan Dic – south and west to the old dyke, or old ditch [054202]. The old ditch probably marked an ancient boundary, such as the parish boundary here, but its precise location is uncertain.

Ond swa west with than Heafdan th'hit cymth to thaere Ealdan Dune – and west along the headland till you come to the old down [041215]. The perambulation would now follow the contours to the old down. The place name Elsdown, as in Elsdown Covert, is a corruption of 'ealden dune' – the old down, and refers to a smoothly rounded low hill.

Andlang Dune west th'hit cymth into Dina More – west along the down till you come to Dina's moor. There is no trace of marshy land here today.

Of ... into Hehstanes Pytte – on to the stone pit, or Hehstanes pit [047219]. One of several possible stone quarries.

Of ... eastward bi tham Heafdan to tham Haethenan Byrigelse with Heallinga Weallan – and eastwards along the headland to the heathen burial by Hawling wall [055218]. The heathen burial would be a tumulus or a long barrow and there is a tumulus located near to the wall marking Hawling's parish boundary. This site can be located with certainty.

Swa east ofer than Sealt Straet to tham Crundaelan' - and east over the Salt Way to the quarry [068221]. The Salt Way is east of the tumulus and a possible quarry lies beyond it. The Salt Way is an old packhorse road along which salt was carried from Droitwich to Lechlade, from where it was taken by boat to London. The reference to the Salt Way in this charter is an indication of the antiquity of this road.

Of ... bi than Heafdan to thaes Bernes Ende – and along the headland to the barn's end [073228 or possibly 065231].

The perambulation is now complete. As we have seen some of the markers of the boundary can be located with certainty, others with intelligent guesswork, only a few are impossible to identify today. Whether this land was all pasture at the time of the charter, as 'feld' suggests, is open to debate. Some slopes within the area are certainly too steep for cultivation using modern farming methods and much of the soil is thin and brashy and makes good sheep pasture, but most is under the plough today.

To the north of the village Finberg identified an area described in the charter as Wald or woodland, and if he is correct in his interpretation, the present village of Hawling lies in the centre of the land between the wald and the feld, land that was probably used for arable farming. There

The deserted settlement site at Hawling. The low sun causes the shadows of the earthworks of former closes and houses to be clearly seen.

is field evidence of a much larger village at Hawling in medieval times, for on the north-east side of the village are the earthworks of former houses and closes. Hawling is an example of a shrunken village which probably experienced a reduction of population at the time of the Black Death in the years 1348 to 1350.

The charter gives details of an early walk around the boundary of this particular piece of land. The route is not the same as that of a frequently used footpath, although as we have seen, some sections were early paths. The inclusion of a green way, a mill path and the salt street in this tenth-century charter gives clear evidence of the age of these paths, and the village itself is probably not much older.

In making the perambulation of a Saxon charter, walking from one boundary marker to the next, interest was directed to one side only of the path. In a sense this was also true of another type of perambulation, that of beating the bounds. Beating the bounds began as a medieval practice associated with Rogationtide. Each year on the three days before Ascension Day, rogation processions were held in many rural parishes. Accompanied by hand bells, banners and processional crosses, parishioners and clergy walked around the parish boundary, beating boundary markers with rods. The boundary was easily accessible because, before the eighteenth-century Parliamentary Enclosure Acts and the earlier formation of small enclosures near the villages, fields were largely open and access to and along the parish boundary was generally unhindered by hedges and walls.

The original purpose of this ceremony was to attempt to drive out from the parish the evil spirits that were thought to cause social division and sickness. Because it was presumed that the evil spirits crossed over the boundary into the neighbouring parishes, when two processions in adjoining parishes came together, each concerned with the removal of the evil spirits from their own parish, the meeting sometimes led to blows! But there was more to Rogation than this. In the 1630s, the parish priest and poet George Herbert in his poem *The Country Parson*, cuts though these superstitions and neatly summarises the purpose of rogation processions into four. These were the blessing of the fields, praying for good weather and abundant harvests; the ensuring of justice in the demarkation of the parish boundaries; the encouragement of charitable relationships between people as they walked together; and the creation of an opportunity for the more wealthy parishioners to give relief to the poor in the food and ale provided for the participants. At specific points along the perambulation crosses of wood or stone were erected and, at each cross, an extract from one of the gospels was read. It was expected that the whole parish population would participate in Rogation and it was, therefore, a major social and religious event in the life of the community. With such large numbers of people involved on an annual basis, it is likely that the rogation paths would have been sufficiently trampled to leave an indelible mark on the ground, in other words the boundary line would have been a beaten way.

Again, as we will see with pilgrimages, rogation processions had been viewed with some concern in the sixteenth century. Some writers of the time expressed the view that junketing and the jostling for position in the processions were inappropriate forms of behaviour for a serious occasion such as this, and that the gospels could be heard more clearly within the church buildings than out in the fields! But some form of rogation procession continued in many rural parishes. At Alvington there has been a token rogation walk in recent years and some of the old ceremonial has been retained or recovered in other rural parishes with processions to the church from different points in the village.

Rogation processions and the delimitation of land areas in Saxon charters are two examples of perambulations and the term is still in limited use today. The boundary of the Forest of Dean has always been referred to as a perambulation and sometimes walks around towns to inspect the urban architecture, as in the Pevsner series on the *Buildings of England*, are described as perambulations. Although the term implies a walk through an area of land, it has the sense of including all that is encompassed by a boundary walk.

For further reading: G.B. Grundy *Saxon Charters of Gloucestershire* BGAS, 1935.

TWO

Pilgrim Ways

In medieval times a pilgrimage to a shrine or other sacred place was a desirable and popular activity. Many people travelled abroad on pilgrimages. Jerusalem and the sites associated with Jesus' life were the most important overseas destinations, but Rome, Compostela and the burial places of saints such as those of St Francis at Assissi and St Boniface at Fulda in Hesse were also frequently visited, even by people from Gloucestershire. Until its recent loss, there was a small-fifteenth century roundel of St James of Compostela in a window of Syde church, presumably commemorating a visit to that shrine in northern Spain. Similarly, the fourteenth-century wall paintings in Stoke Orchard church, portraying the life of St James, may have been commissioned by another pilgrim on returning from a journey there. Also, beside the south door and at the south-west corner of this small Norman church are incised crosses. These are thought to have been made by pilgrims as they stopped for prayer on their journey to Compostela, and some have circles around the ends of the crosses, perhaps added after their safe return. As nearby Bristol was the port of departure for pilgrimages to Spain, many people coming from the Midlands and the north of England would have passed this way.

In England, the tomb of St Thomas Becket at Canterbury was the primary destination for pilgrimages, but there were many other important shrines. Those at Worcester, Hereford, Oxford and Evesham were particularly popular, attracting many pilgrims, and the four in Gloucestershire had the additional pull of their royal connections. The Gloucestershire shrines were the tomb of St Kenelm in Winchcombe Abbey, the shrine containing relics of St Oswald in St Oswald's Priory in Gloucester, the

Above: The twelfth-century church at Stoke Orchard. The interior walls are covered with paintings portraying the life of St James.

Left: Pilgrim marks scratched into the wall by the south door of St James the Great church, Stoke Orchard.

shrine of the Holy Blood at Hailes Abbey and the tomb of King Edward II in Gloucester Cathedral. Shrines were usually located near the high altar of their respective churches, and the later ones were arched structures, with space beneath for offerings and into which pilgrims could reach to touch the shrine and to pray. The bones or relics of the saint were usually held on top, sometimes in gold, silver and jewelled chests. The relics of St Oswald and the Holy Blood at Hailes were probably housed in this way.

As Chaucer's *Canterbury Tales* indicate, people from many sections of society undertook these journeys. Many were desperately seeking supernatural help and miracle cures. For the latter, detailed information is sometimes available when the healing miracles were associated with the relics of a person who was being examined for canonisation. In these cases descriptions of the particular ailments and cures were carefully noted by the commissioners who had been appointed by the pope to assess the prospective saint's life, and these records are still held in the Vatican. It has been possible to translate some of the illnesses into modern medical terms, and although no research has been published on the reputed cures at the Gloucestershire shrines, it has for that of Thomas Cantilupe, a thirteenth-century Bishop of Hereford. This research shows that people were prepared to travel long distances in the hope of a cure. Thus in 1303 William de Lonsdale pushed his fifteen-year-old daughter, Alice, in a one-wheeled cart from London to Hereford to the tomb of Thomas Cantilupe for the apparently successful healing of a ten-year-old foot injury and painful infection. They travelled through Gloucestershire on their journey, and therefore passed by a number of alternative shrines with their own reputations for healing. Some of the reported healings are very similar to present day faith healings, and especially to those recorded from remote parts of the world where modern medicine has not yet fully penetrated. But some reported cures would not be recognised as such today, and many of the ailments cured were psychogenic. The existence of shrines not only inspired hope for cures from a variety of ills, they also reinforced the popular desire for the particular saint's support both in this life and the life to come. Attendant monks prayed for the pilgrims and used the best medical skills available at the time for healing and care, being mindful of the significance of their successes to the reputations of both saints and shrines. There was evidently some competition between the shrines for attracting the visits of pilgrims.

Pilgrimages were not only undertaken for healing. Some were made out of gratitude for a special favour, such as the birth of a son or the preservation of life in a time of famine or plague, others were simply acts of devotion to God. Sometimes they were voluntary expressions of penitence for wrongdoing. Later in the Middle Ages the courts occasionally ordered a pilgrimage as a punishment for a criminal offence, and then a less savoury element was brought into the company of pilgrims. Pilgrimages provided the opportunity for experiencing, for a fixed and limited time, some of the disciplines and hardships of a monastic life. They were often understood as being symbolic of life's pilgrimage, enabling the pilgrim to see his or her life in a wider context than the parochial, to which it was normally restricted. This was achieved by introducing the pilgrim to new places and to new people from a variety of different backgrounds, and so to new perspectives on life. There was also an element of early tourism in pilgrimages and the journeys were not without dangers and risks, especially if they involved overseas travel. For this reason they often appealed to the more adventurous members of the medieval population. Pilgrims often travelled in groups and were sometimes accompanied by a guide. Their desired route was followed in

The galleried courtyard of the New Inn, Gloucester, built around 1450 to accommodate pilgrims.

stages, with directions being given from one resting place such as an inn or a monastery to the next.

We begin with the visits to a shrine which survived the destructions of the sixteenth century, the tomb of Edward II. Because of Gloucester's geographical position, most fourteenth- and fifteenth-century pilgrims to the city would have come from the north and east and would have entered through the North Gate. Once inside the city, many would have sought accommodation at the New Inn. According to Robert Cole's *Rental of the Houses of Gloucester* dated 1455, this inn had been recently built for St Peter's Abbey by one of its monks, John de Twyning, and it has been assumed that its main purpose was to house pilgrims. It had the capacity to accommodate up to 200 at a time. With its galleried courtyard the New Inn is a remarkable survivor from the mid-fifteenth century. The adjective 'new' in its name indicates that it had replaced an earlier inn on the same site, and there were others in Gloucester at the time.

From the New Inn, pilgrims would have walked along Northgate Street, past the cordwainers making shoes, belts and other leather items, perhaps equipping themselves for the return journey, and then into Westgate Street. This was the principal market street of the city. Woollen and silk goods were sold in the Mercery on the north side of the street, and on the south was the Butchery. There was a cluster of buildings in the middle of the street, which included the butter and cheese market, later known as the King's Board, and two churches. Narrow burgage plots abutted the street and the half-timbered, jettied houses had their gable ends to the street. The cathedral precincts could be entered by the public through two gateways, on the west side St Mary's Gate dates from 1190 and on the south side was King Edward's Gate. After the 1450s the soaring 225ft-high cathedral tower would have dominated the view of Gloucester for miles around, but from the latter gate the pilgrims would have gained their first view of the south front of the cathedral with its notable ballflower decoration and finely sculptured figures. If they had travelled from the nearby villages of Badgeworth or Bishop's Cleeve, or had visited Winchcombe Abbey and admired its stonework, they may have seen ballflowers before, but for most visitors it would have been a new experience.

Entering the cathedral by the west door, pilgrims passed along the south aisle by the massive Norman pillars. These are 30ft high and 21ft feet in circumference and still convey an impression of solidity, stability and strength, in contrast to the delicacy of the outside stonework. Climbing the steps into the ambulatory, the pilgrims would have been led round to the north-east side, and so to King Edward II's tomb.

Edward's life-sized effigy is carved in alabaster, and although it is stylized, there is character in the facial expression. It is one of the earliest alabaster effigies and became influential for effigy carving elsewhere. It rests on a table tomb of oolitic limestone and this is clad in Purbeck marble, at that time a stone symbolic of royalty. The Purbeck limestone is also finely carved, and the whole tomb is under a very complex and light, two-staged canopy of oolitic limestone, intricate in its workmanship. A small area of the original medieval floor tiles still remains at its base. The Norman piers beside the tomb have been bevelled to frame it and on them a band of rusty brown has been painted with a decorative pattern of white harts, commemorating a visit to the tomb by Richard II in 1378. Edward's alabaster crown was once adorned with jewels and small holes mark their former positions. Niches in the sides of the tomb show where dowells were used to attach figures of weepers.

This was the shrine to which pilgrims came in large numbers from about 1330. The *Historia* of the abbey says that within a few years of Edward's burial 'there was such a crowd of the common people that the city of Gloucester scarcely held the multitude of people flowing together there from various cities of England, towns, villages and hamlets'. The gifts of these pilgrims were subsequently important for the building programme of the cathedral and contributed to the rebuilding of the south transept (1331-6) and the choir and presbytery (1337-67), where the Perpendicular style of architecture was first displayed outside London.

Walking round the ambulatory, the pilgrim's eyes would rise to the ruby, blue, yellow and translucent white glass of the great east window. The lower lights of this window contain the arms of those who fought at Crecy in 1346, above them are the figures of earlier abbots and bishops, then saints and martyrs, then Christ, Mary and the apostles, and finally towards the top, angels. At each stage the canopies above the figures get taller. The stone tracery of the window and the perpendicular shafts of the reshaped Norman piers fan out to the complex lierne vault roof above, and at each intersection of the ribs of the vault is a boss. Nineteen of these bosses are in the form of a carved angel, most of whom play a musical instrument, and the central boss shows Christ in glory, his right hand raised in blessing and his left hand holding the orb of the world.

The ruins of St Oswald's Priory, Gloucester. Some of the relics of St Oswald were enshrined here in 909.

The window was the greatest in medieval Europe, as large as a tennis court, and it has a setting to match. Here near the climax of the pilgrimage the company of pilgrims would sense that they had been joined in worship by the company of heaven.

It is not exactly clear why Edward's tomb became a medieval shrine. Possibly the cruelty of his treatment and brutal murder at Berkeley Castle was a factor. Edward III certainly fostered the interest in his father's tomb, and miracles were claimed here. Incidentally, the existence of the King's tomb probably saved the cathedral from destruction at the Dissolution – in contrast to that of the other great abbeys at Hailes, Winchcombe and Cirencester.

There had also been an earlier royal shrine in Gloucester. This dates from about the year 909, when Ethelfleda, daughter of King Alfred, arranged for some of the bones of St Oswald to be brought to Gloucester from their temporary resting place at Bardney in Lincolnshire. They were then placed in her newly founded minster, which later became St Oswald's Priory. St Oswald had been king of Northumbria, re-establishing Christianity there in the seventh century, and was martyred.

His body was savagely cut to pieces to obliterate his memory but various parts were obtained by his followers and taken to different places in the country, where they were treasured as relics. And so the cult of St Oswald was spread in this unforeseen way. His head went to Durham, an arm to Peterborough and most of the remainder to Gloucester. The shrine of a royal saint was of great importance and St Oswald's was especially so, since he was not only the first of them, but was one who was revered both for his life and his death. Documentary evidence of pilgrimages to St Oswald's shrine suddenly and inexplicably ceases after 1161. This probably reflects the trend for visits to shrines associated with saints to be replaced by visits to shrines dedicated to Mary or in a few cases to Jesus – to move from 'the spiritual middle-men toward the heart of Christianity' as Ronald Finucane put it, and the next destination of pilgrimage also illustrates this trend.

Hailes was one of the last great Cistercian abbeys to be founded in Britain and the abbey church was dedicated in 1251. It was built to fulfil a vow made by Richard, Earl of Cornwall and brother to Henry III, in thanksgiving for deliverance from a storm at sea. The original lay out of the abbey and church followed the traditional Cistercian plan. Then in 1270, Richard's son, Edmund, acquired a reputed sample of the blood of Christ, which had been given patriarchal authentification. This he presented to Hailes. To accommodate such a relic, the eastern end of the church was rebuilt into a chevet with five chapels, rather like the layout of the apse of Tewkesbury Abbey, and a shrine of gold, silver and precious stones was made to house the glass flask containing the blood. The shrine was dedicated with much ceremony in 1277. Painted boards, telling the story of the acquisition of the blood and the miracles associated with it, were hung near the shrine, and its wooden cover could be raised to show the relic, as is demonstrated in an old drawing.

Today, the former position of the shrine and the footings of the chevet are marked out on the ground, and a photograph of the seal of the Confraternity of Hailes, displayed in the museum, shows a monk holding the glass flask containing the Holy Blood. For nearly 300 years the shrine became the most popular destination for pilgrimage in Gloucestershire. In 1533 Hugh Latimer wrote in a letter from his home at West Kington near the Wiltshire/Gloucestershire border, 'I dwell within a mile of the Foss Way and you would wonder how they come by flocks out of the West country to Our Lady of Worcester but chiefly to the Blood of

The ruins of the Cistercian abbey church at Hailes. The shrine of the Holy Blood was on the small grassy mound just left of centre.

Hailes which they believe the very sight of it puts them in a state of salvation'. Chaucer's *Pardoner's Tale* also refers to 'the Blood of Christ that is in Hailes' and many pamphlets were produced encouraging visits to the shrine.

The small parish church at Hailes was soon adopted by the abbey, becoming a *capella ante portas* (chapel by the gate), and later visitors to it would have been impressed by its wall paintings, which include on the north wall a giant figure of St Christopher, the patron saint of travellers. After entering the abbey precincts the main entrance to the church could be found at its west end. The walk from here to the shrine would take in the full length of the church, some 135 paces, but it has been suggested that pilgrims may have had access through the north transept, past Richard's tomb, and thence to the shrine.

Cistercians normally chose quiet, remote places for their monasteries. Hailes did not exactly fulfil these requirements, so the existing village population was moved to Didbrook in order to create more favourable conditions for the monks. It was also unusual for a Cistercian monastery to receive such a large number of visitors. There was a pilgrims' inn where Pilgrim House stands today, but accommodation at Hailes was naturally limited. At Winchcombe, however, the Benedictine abbey buildings could also take pilgrims. Here the former George Inn was an inn for pilgrims. Rebuilt in the early sixteenth century by the abbey, it still retains the initials R.K. in the spandrels of the timber door frame. R.K. stands for Richard Kidderminster, the penultimate abbot who resigned in 1525. Abbot's House a little further along the High Street may also have accommodated pilgrims, and a much-weathered corbel bearing the coat of arms of the abbey is beneath its oriel window.

So the path between Winchcombe and Hailes was much used as a way for pilgrims. As they walked such paths, pilgrims would have thought about the significance of their visits and in this case about the blood of Christ that they anticipated seeing shortly. Royalty had used the path at the original dedication of Hailes Abbey and Edmund followed it before presenting the Holy Blood. Later, gifts were made 'to amend the way', for example by Sir John Huddleston in 1512. Strangely, today it is one of the least interesting sections of the Cotswold Way, sun-baked and soil-cracked in summer and wet and muddy in winter, and in the higher sheep-grazed stretch the alignment of the path is not very clear, although there is a slight levelling of the surface. At either end the path leads into lanes, Puckpit Lane at the Winchcombe end and Salters Lane at Hailes. The tracks that descend from the Cotswolds to Hailes, which were the routes usually taken by the majority of pilgrims that Latimer mentions, were well maintained and one still retains signs of a carefully cobbled construction. The gifts made by pilgrims at Hailes, as in the case of Gloucester, helped to maintain the fabric of this magnificent building – to which the beautifully carved bosses in the museum bear witness.

Compared with those at Gloucester and Hailes, less is known about the other shrine, that of St Kenelm. Kenelm was the son of the Mercian king, Kenulf, who founded Winchcombe Abbey in 798. The legends associated with St Kenelm grew around his murder in around 811 on the slopes of the Clent Hills, north of Romsley in Worcestershire, and the stages in the transport of his body to Winchcombe. A sacred well just below St Kenelm's church at Romsley marks the reputed place of the murder. His shrine at Winchcombe was probably in the abbey church, although there has been speculation that it may have been just outside the present east end of the parish church. When the abbey became a Benedictine house in 969, it was dedicated to St Mary and St Kenelm. This shrine also attracted many visi-

The Pilgrim Way between Winchcombe and Hailes. This path linked the shrines in both abbeys.

tors and in the early twelfth century William of Malmesbury wrote:

> The body of the little saint is very generally adored, and there is hardly any place in England more venerated, or where greater numbers of persons attend at the festival (July 17th), and this arising from the long-continued belief of his sanctity and the constant exhibition of miracles.

A visit to a shrine of a child saint was then popular with parents who had lost their own children at a young age. Here at Winchcombe pilgrims also contributed to the wealth of the abbey. There is no trace of the shrine today as the abbey was rapidly and completely destroyed at the Dissolution, its stone going mainly to Sudeley Castle, although a few houses in Winchcombe such as Rabbit Box Cottage have carved pieces. The two centres associated with St Kenelm, Romsley and Winchcombe were linked by a popular pilgrim route, which mostly follows the Salt Way.

Pilgrims often bought badges at a shrine as souvenirs of their visit and attached them to their hats. There were badges from Jerusalem and Rome and a scallop shell for a hat badge was the sign of a visit to Compostela. The Corinium Museum in Cirencester displays three pewter pilgrim

St Kenelm's Well on the hillside east of Winchcombe. Inscriptions on the interior walls of the stone building give details of the well's history.

badges and one is thought to be from the shrine of St Kenelm.

In addition to the four shrines, there were also sacred wells in Gloucestershire. Along the route taken by the monks transporting St Kenelm's body were several. They include St Kenelm's Well on the hillside above Sudeley Castle, where the Victorian well housing built by Emma Dent displaced an Elizabethan conduit and probably an earlier sacred well. A blocked-up window from the earlier structure is incorporated in the back wall of the nearby house. A plaque within the well housing gives some details of its history. These sacred wells had reputed healing properties for skin and eye complaints, as with St Edward's Well, now overgrown and inaccessible close to the Fosse Way south of Stow-on-the-Wold, and St Anthony's Well, shaded beneath the beech trees near Greenbottom in the Forest of Dean. Visits to the wells continued long after the Dissolution of the monasteries had taken place. The water from a spring symbolised something everlasting, with cleansing and refreshing properties, and also life and death, the medium without which life cannot exist and within which human life is impossible. Much of this imagery was drawn from the Bible.

Concerned voices had been raised during the Middle Ages about the excesses associated with pilgrimages, the authenticity of the relics and the idolatry of worshipping saints. John Wycliffe, as early as the fourteenth century, preached against the acquisition of great wealth by the custodians of the shrines, 'God gave his sheep to be pastured, not to be shaven and shorn', he said. Thomas à Kempis warned against pilgrimages in his *Imitation of Christ* of 1418. The *Augsburg Confession* of 1530 referred to them as 'childish and useless works' and many of the reformers spoke against them and their associated papal indulgences. Henry VIII used as an argument for the Dissolution of the monasteries the invalidity of their relics and their excess of wealth. The *Forty-two Articles* declared that the worshipping 'of images, as of reliques, and also invocation of sainctes, is a fonde thing vainlie feigned, and grounded upon no warraunt of scripture'. Moreover pilgrimages were sometimes seen as playing into the hands of corrupt abbots, who regarded them as an easy way of making money from gullible visitors. Piles of abandoned crutches beside the shrine could be most impressive! So, with a series of orders against them, a time came during the Reformation when pilgrimages were completely banned. The commissioners of Thomas Cromwell, working for Henry VIII, demolished the shrines and scattered their bones and other relics, as between 1535 and 1538 they visited the monasteries to assess their wealth. By 1540 the monasteries had gone.

Nevertheless, the financial contributions of generations of pilgrims and of royalty to the upkeep of the shrines, and therefore to the development of medieval architecture, was immense. The broadening of outlook resulting from a pilgrimage must also have affected society. The development of spas in the seventeenth and eighteenth centuries, to which people travelled for health reasons, in some respects parallels the establishment of shrines in medieval times and in this sense served a similar purpose. Recently there has been a renewed interest in pilgrimages and visits to sacred places, which the tourist industry has encouraged, and visitors to sacred wells may sometimes see small pieces of cloth tied to nearby trees which mark the end of a modern pilgrimage as at Romsley.

For further reading: Ronald Finucane *Miracles and Pilgrims, Popular Beliefs in Medieval England*, Dent 1977.

THREE

Marching to War

As far back as Iron Age times, and probably long before, the land now forming Gloucestershire has experienced some kind of warfare. The stonework of the ramparts of the Iron Age hill forts along the Cotswold escarpment at Crickley and Leckhampton Hills has been reddened by fire, as the wooden superstructures were set alight by hostile invaders. The straight Roman roads across the county were designed to allow soldiers to quickly reach trouble spots. There were important battles at Dyrham in 577 and at Tewkesbury in 1471, and in the seventeenth century the Civil War affected the whole area.

The causes of the English Civil War in the 1640s are complex, and even the participants were frequently unclear about the reasons for it, as they joined coalitions of varied interests. Their motivation included anger at the long period during which Parliament had been dissolved and the country ruled by the royal court, opposition to Charles I's method of raising ship money to strengthen the navy, a fear of the spreading influence of Catholicism via the court and a dislike of some of archbishop William Laud's policies to restore church ritual. Laud was already unpopular in Gloucester, where he had been Dean between 1616 and 1621. In his concern for reverence and dignity in church services he had ordered the communion table to be moved to the east end of the choir, so making it less accessible to the people, and had requested that the clergy and other church officials bow before it on entering the choir. To the puritan mind this smacked too much of popery, although this was not Laud's intention.

Generally, the Church, large land-owning families and the rural poor supported the King, while the town merchants, tradesmen and the people employed in industrial work supported Parliament. However, the choice of sides was not always easy and many wrestled with their consciences over the matter. Reading the recently printed King James version of the Bible did not clarify matters, for on the one hand loyalty to the King was encouraged by such texts as 'My son, fear thou the Lord and the king: and meddle not with them that are given to change' from the *Proverbs*, and 'Fear God. Honour the king' from *1 Peter*. On the other hand the perception that religious statues, paintings and stained-glass windows were idolatrous, and therefore contrary to the second commandment, was common among the Parliamentarians. There were also worries over the country's stability and civil order if Charles was overthrown, but at the same time a strong revulsion at the excesses of the King. 'The measures of the king and his ministers were entertained with disaffection by a considerable majority of the population', was a view expressed in Gloucestershire. However, once war had started the decision as to which side to support had to be made quickly by many people.

None of the great battles of the Civil War took place in Gloucestershire, although Edgehill in Warwickshire was not far away, but the War's impact was felt throughout the county. 'The whole of its surface was long exposed to the miseries of petty and desultory warfare', wrote James Washbourne, a later commentator, and there are still visible signs of that warfare in the landscape today. There were Royalist strongholds at Berkeley, Sudeley, Beverstone, Lydney and other seats of gentry, and troops were conscripted at these places from the local population, a population which was often very dependent on the Royalist families. But Gloucester and the larger towns such as Cirencester and Tewkesbury, and the centres of the woollen industry around Stroud, were Parliamentarian with a strong puritan interest. The population of the Forest of Dean, incensed at Sir John Winter's oppressive iron-working operations, was also generally anti-Royalist. So the county's population was divided and uneasy. It was also vulnerable. Charles had his headquarters at Oxford, and Gloucestershire was positioned between these and his supporters in Wales and parts of the south-west of England and Gloucester itself, as the lowest fixed bridge point of the Severn, was strategically located. The Cotswold woollen mills were required to supply cloth for the uniforms of both armies, frequently of the same colour, and likewise the iron industry of the Forest of Dean was the source of cannons and cannon balls for both sides. So inevitably there were numerous local skirmishes

The ruins of Campden House, destroyed in 1645. At the far end of the terrace a pavilion has been recently restored by the Landmark Trust.

Marks of Civil War gun shot may still be seen on the west wall of Winchcombe church.

between the armies, as well as the important sieges of Cirencester and Gloucester. One small skirmish, which has left a burial mound of soldiers' bodies, was at Chapel Farm, Redmarley.

Armies marched through the county in all four years of fighting, requiring food and shelter on their journeys. Some provisions were paid for, but much was simply plundered. Pillaging was common, livestock were killed for food, crops were damaged and the local population left starving and impoverished after an army had passed through their neighbourhood. Sometimes compensation was received after the war, for example in 1647 John Chamberlayne of Maugersbury received £36 – the value of four loads of wheat, eight loads of beans and fourteen loads of hay, which had been supplied to the local garrison. But many providers received nothing. The agricultural markets were disrupted, roads and bridges were damaged by the passage of heavy ammunition wagons and guns, and there was much destruction of property. Campden House, which had only been completed in 1620 at a reputed cost of £29,000, was burnt to the ground in 1645, the same year that Sir John Winter also deliberately destroyed White Cross, his house at Lydney, lest it should come into Parliamentarian hands. Sudeley Castle was slighted and left as a ruin in 1649, and likewise Beverstone Castle was damaged in 1644 and Berkeley Castle in 1645. Where sieges had taken place many town houses were deliberately demolished to allow for easier military manoeuvres. The walls of churches such as those at Painswick and Winchcombe are still pock marked from cannon or musket fire. Church art, both in stained-glass windows such as those in the cloisters of Gloucester Cathedral, and in sculptures and paintings, often the product of skilled craftsmanship and of exquisite design, was deliberately and ruthlessly vandalised. Even market crosses were demolished in the iconoclasm. A few place names are also reminders of the events of the time. 'Bloody Jim' is a field near Upper Swell, 'Shoot Hill' is at Ruardean and 'Gore Brook' is a stream below Edge Hills near Cinderford. The War sometimes caused divisions within families, as well as between neighbours and friends. It was a tragic, terrifying and costly period in this country's history, but it had very significant consequences and is sometimes viewed as the most formative event in the fashioning of the English nation.

In this chapter we will consider the routes taken by soldiers as they prepared for warfare and the impact they had on the lands they passed through. There are several well-documented journeys we could follow. These include the various raids on Royalist garrisons by the troops of Colonel Massey from his base in Gloucester, which involved skirmishes at Westbury, Littledean and Newnham; the mopping up operations of Sir William Waller's army on both sides of the lower Severn and the route taken by the army under the Earl of Essex, coming from London for the relief of Gloucester. These were all movements of Parliamentarian armies, and the routes they took depended not only on their military objectives but also on the security of the route from likely Royalist attacks and the ease of movement in the particular conditions of ground surface and weather at the time. The journey for which the most detailed documentation exists is that made by Henry Foster and his fellow soldiers. Foster was a sergeant in the red regiment, one of the two regiments of trained soldiers, which together with three raw auxiliary regiments marched to the relief of Gloucester after the city had been put under siege on 10th August 1643. His report of the march has been preserved in *Bibliotheca Gloucestrensis*. The account is one-sided, clearly designed for propaganda purposes and written from a limited perspective, but it gives the day-to- day experiences of one soldier and his colleagues as they marched towards Gloucester to challenge Charles I's army and expected to be involved in military action at any moment. A summary of the report of the journey follows, together with more detailed comment on the experiences of the red regiment as it passed through Gloucestershire.

Foster writes that the march from London began on Wednesday 23 August 1643, a fortnight after the siege had started, and that the regiment reached Brainsford at 1 a.m. early the next morning. Troops were often moved at night. He says that many citizens then returned to London and hired others to replace them! They had already found that the rhetoric of war did not quite match the reality. On the Friday they moved on to Uxbridge, and on the Saturday to Chaffin (Chalfont). Here the first casualty occurred, when a soldier was accidentally shot by a musketeer on the same side. On Sunday, 27 August, the red regiment was joined by both the blue regiment and the auxiliaries on a great common three miles from Chessun (Chesham). Foster's own regiment was quartered at the house of a Mr Cheyney, plenty of beer was provided, and between 200 and 300 men slept there in a barn.

On the next day they marched to Asson-Clinton (Aston Clinton) where they stayed for two nights, and then they moved to Clayden

(Claydon). This was a day of fasting, one of many, and as they passed Alesbury (Aylesbury) great guns were fired at every fort around the town. The red regiment was quartered at the home of Sir Ralph Verney, who was a Parliamentarian, though his father, Sir Edmund Verney, who had been killed at Edgehill the previous year, had been the King's standard bearer. This was one of the many examples of sadly divided families. Claydon House is still the home of the Verney family. On Thursday 31 August, they reached Stretton-Ardley (Stratton Audley), where the whole brigade was quartered. This meant that about 5,000 men were here, with little provision because the Cavaliers had been in the district the previous night, a sequence of events that was repeated on more than one occasion on the march. At Baynard's Green on the next day, amid great shouting and triumph, the brigade met the lord general's army. (The lord general was the Earl of Essex). Foster reports that it was 'a goodly and glorious sight' to see the whole army of horse and foot together, at least 15,000 men. The brigade then moved on to Souldern, while the rest of the army was a mile away at Ano on the hill (Aynho). They were 'very much scanted of victualls in this place'. On Saturday, 2 September, they were at Hook Norton and on the Sunday they reached Addington (Oddington), one mile from Stow the Old (Stow-on-the-Wold), having again briefly met up with Essex's army on a great common near Chipping Norton. The spelling of place names varies in the document and was evidently based on how the names sounded to Foster as he recalled them from memory. There were then no road signs to read, nor were mileages accurate.

They were now in Gloucestershire, and the night at Oddington was a miserable one. The blue regiment had reached the village first and found quarters, presumably in Lower Oddington, and the auxiliaries had looked for their quarters in adjacent villages, which may have included Adlestrop, although the Leighs at Adlestrop like the Chamberlaynes at Maugersbury were Royalists. So the red regiment had to go on a further half-mile and was now in the front. The soldiers had just settled when an alarm was raised. Consequently they had to stand on guard all night in a field, without bread or water and having had no food the previous day, with the main army still three miles away at Chipping Norton, and without accurate intelligence of the whereabouts of the Cavaliers. It was also a very cold night and they dared not light a fire. This is an interesting comment on the weather at the time. The mid-seventeenth century is sometimes known as the Little Ice Age, with temperatures at their lowest for a millennium, and significantly lower than today's. A fire was usually necessary on the frosty nights of early September, for autumn had already arrived.

Between Oddington and Stow-on-the-Wold the red regiment had a merciful escape. On Monday 3 September, having obtained some refreshment, they were alerted to the fact that the enemy was near and that they were in a vulnerable position in the little open village. So they marched into a broad spacious field towards the top of a hill, where they found that they were surrounded by 4-5,000 enemy cavalry. Some were in front of them, higher up and less than a quarter-mile away, some were in the Evenlode valley to their right, and some were climbing the hill to their rear. The regiment was completely cut off from the rest of the army, and a message describing their plight was conveyed to Essex. They then lined the hedges with musketeers, and after defiantly facing the enemy for half-an-hour, they tried to provoke an attack by firing one or two shots at them and by sending a few horsemen brandishing swords to within firing range. But there was no responding attack and soon some auxiliary forces brought reinforcements to the isolated regiment.

The countryside near Stow-on-the-Wold from the east. At the time of the Civil War the fields near the hill top were open, those in the Evenlode Valley were enclosed.

Stow-on-the-Wold church. 1600 Royalist prisoners were held here. The stone near the foot of the tower also commemorates the battle.

Eventually there was the welcome sight of Essex's army descending the hill, one-and-a-half miles behind them. The arriving army fired three or four drakes (small cannon) and the enemy cavalry retreated.

The combined force then marched up the hill towards the Royalist horsemen. Some drakes were fired at them, and again there was an enemy retreat. Then, in a further confrontation, two 'great pieces of ordnance' were fired at them, and they retreated to Stow-on-the-Wold. The greatest ordnance was then employed, and the enemy was pursued for three miles. Skirmishes continued to 9 p.m. and the pursuit to 12 a.m. Five or six regiments were involved in the pursuit, soldiers marching 800 to 1,000 abreast and six men deep. There was room for this impressive display of strength because it was 'brave champian country'. This number of soldiers abreast, each man carrying his weapon, means that the line was at least half-a-mile across. Interestingly, the report indicates that some of the Evenlode valley must have been enclosed to give the hedges along which the musketeers moved, while nearer to Stow-on-the-Wold there were large open arable fields.

One man was lost in the first skirmish, 'slain by our own cannon through his negligence, and another was sore burnt and hurt by the same piece' — an indication of the unreliability of the guns. Foster adds that at Stow-on-the-Wold the Cavaliers had reported that they had killed twenty of his men and had lost only two of their own, but 'we hear of six of theirs slain, horses killed and five prisoners taken'. He found out that Prince Rupert had been there and possibly other key Royalist leaders. That night they lay in an open ploughed field, with no straw and no bread and water, 'yet cheerful and with no feeble sick person among them'. However, John Chamberlayne claimed later that the cost of providing bread, beer, cheese, meat and provinder to at least some of Essex' army came to £6, in addition to the trampling of his corn valued at £40. Stow-on-the-Wold, high on the hill top, was in a commanding position and fighting returned to it again in March 1646. The final battle of the War took place on the undulating country north of Stow-on-the-Wold, and recently a monument to this battle has been erected on the hillside west of Donnington. In that battle 1,600 Royalists were taken prisoner. Stow church was used to hold them and there is a memorial slab on the chancel floor to Hastings Keyt of Ebrington, one of the captains killed then. It was a common practice to keep prisoners in churches, as these were the largest and most secure buildings at the time. The churches

Prestbury Hill down which the red regiment took the cannons and ammunition on its way to the relief of Gloucester.

at Burford, Cirencester, Painswick, St Mary de Lode in Gloucester and Winchcombe also held prisoners at different times of the War. No doubt their fabric suffered considerably, and the church at Stow was described as ruinous in 1657.

On the Tuesday they continued their march via Naunton and Brockhampton to Prestbury Hill, with the red regiment at the rear in charge of the wagons. Reaching the top of this 'high mountain or hill', Essex ordered that four or five great pieces of ordnance should be fired. Foster was unclear whether this was to warn off the Cavaliers in the valley below or to inform Gloucester of the approaching relief. Gloucester is visible from Prestbury Hill, but some reports suggest that the wind was in the wrong direction and the cannon was not heard there. No doubt those looking out from the cathedral tower would have seen signs of the approach. The army then marched down the hill to find quarters in the villages at the foot, while Essex moved on to Cheltenham for accommodation. Cheltenham was described as a market town and the Royalists had to be removed first. Meanwhile the red regiment was left on the hill with the wagons. Attempts had been made to move some wagons down 'the very craggy steep and dangerous hill' in the darkness and a number were overturned with damage to the carriages and death to the horses. So the regiment stayed all night on the hill. 'It being a most terrible tempestuous night of winde and raine as ever men lay out in, we having neither hedge nor tree for shelter, nor any sustenance of food, or fire', and every soldier had to stand on guard all night. The regiment had marched for six days with little provision as no place was able to provide this. It had 'left the road all the way and marched through poor little villages'. No wonder that the next day, after coming down from the hill, wet to their skins and unable to find refreshments because every house was already full of soldiers and the Cavaliers had been there the previous day, they complained pitifully. The red and blue regiments then found reasonable accommodation and refreshments at Norton, four miles from Gloucester, where despite many alarms they stayed for two days and nights. Coming from London, which by Stuart times had many impressive buildings, the Cotswold villages would have seemed poor to Foster and his assessment of the terrain suggests a flat Fenland upbringing! But even today in stormy conditions and at night, it would be difficult to bring heavy horse-drawn artillery over the edge of the Cotswold escarpment. The bleakness, lack of shelter, wind exposure and driving rain on Cleeve Hill can be easily imagined. It is also interesting to notice that the troops did not follow the main roads. The land use of the Cotswolds was then mainly in sheep pasture and open downland, and such land was much easier to march across than it would have been in post-Enclosure times, when stone walls would have been built and hedges planted – although the Royalist cavalry would not have found the latter to be major obstacles.

Meanwhile on Thursday 7 September, the King's forces attacked a troop of Parliamentarian horsemen at Winscombe (Winchcombe), killing many men, taking some as prisoners and also capturing some colours.

Then, on the 8 September, Essex marched into Gloucester. The city had been besieged for one month and three days, suffering many assaults and batterings. Its walls had been undermined in two or three places, as had its East Gate, and many 'granadoes had been shot into the city – red as fire'. Granadoes were explosive incendiary shells. No one had been killed by them, they only 'tore up the ground as if a beare had been rooting up the earth'. However, Foster reported that about thirty Gloucester people had lost their lives in the siege, 'mostly shot in the head while peeping through holes at the enemy'! Another report said that most were killed by musket fire as they looked over the wall at Friars Orchard. Even entering the city from the north side, the army would have quickly recognised the damage to property. 241 houses had been ruined, together with barns, stables, outhouses and gardens. Most damage had occurred in the south and east wards of the city, with the destruction of eighty-eight and sixty-eight houses, respectively. Only one house still survives of those that had been built outside the South Gate before the siege. The property destruction here had been deliberate in order to prevent the Royalists from approaching the walls of the city under cover. The South Gate itself required rebuilding the next year, when it was given the famous inscriptions 'A city assailed by man, but saved by God' and 'Ever remember the 5th of September, 1643. Give God the glory'. The North Gate, which was then the city's gaol, was also damaged; the top of St Nicholas' church steeple was removed by cannon fire and possibly that of St Mary de Lode as well. The Greyfriars was also battered. The fine city had been scarred. One of the young Welsh soldiers involved in the siege reported that beforehand 'the city was reckoned one of the prettiest towns in England'. Perhaps as many as a third of the population of the city had been made homeless and at the end of the war the total

A distant view of Gloucester from Painswick Beacon. Spoonbed Hill, where the Royalist army camped after the siege, is in the left foreground.

damage to property and contents was valued at £34,000. We may note the comparison with the value of the single Campden House. It has been estimated that 30,000 men were in the King's army besieging the city, whose garrison numbered a mere 1,400.

On Sunday, 10 September, the Parliamentarian army marched north to Tewkesbury. Here it remained for four days and five nights until Gloucester was supplied with the necessary corn and provisions. During the siege the enemy had cut the lead pipes bringing water from Robinswood Hill and diverted the flow of the river Twyver from supplying power to the corn mills. The town of Tewkesbury was summoned to give a twentieth of its estate to relieve Gloucester. Meanwhile the Royalist besieging army had withdrawn to Painswick, stopping here on Spoonbed Hill, before moving to Evesham via the Royalist estates at Coberley and Sudeley.

Henry Foster's report was printed in London on 22 October 1643, within a month of his safe return there. The homeward journey through Cirencester, where the army captured twenty-seven wagon loads of vital Royalist provisions, involved the costly battle of Newbury. He wrote of this battle:

> The enemies canon did play most against the red regiment of trained bands, they did some execution amongst us at the first and were somewhat dreadfull when men's bowels and brains flew in our faces: But blessed bee God that gave us courage, so that we kept our ground.

At one point on this return journey the army drove along about 1,000 sheep and sixty cattle as a future food supply, and eighty-seven sheep were earmarked for the red regiment. But in the warfare they lost them all! Presumably the troops from London had not the skills of the Welsh cattle drovers who followed the same route 100 years later.

There is sufficient detail in Foster's report to retrace the general movement of his regiment, but the precise tracks along which it passed for most of the journey cannot be identified. Marching several soldiers abreast would have required open country and, as he says, they deliberately kept off the roads. However, the troops accompanying the wagons and artillery would have followed roads where possible, while the cavalry moved freely across the fields, much as foxhunters do today. The march from London to Gloucester and back covered more than

200 miles. The soldiers were often desperately short of food, frequently cold and wet and, at least during their travel through Gloucestershire, they had always been vulnerable to attacks from the Royalist army. They would have observed the destruction and waste caused by the military actions. For Foster, his pride in the Parliamentarian army, especially in its red regiment, and a sense of comradeship among the troops, together with the difficulties of finding adequate food and rest, dominated his thoughts on the march, and these are the main themes of the report. In this respect it is probably typical of many military memoirs. Pleasant scenery, flowers and wildlife, varied farming practices and the changing rural architecture of southern England, topics that have often interested walkers crossing the county at other times, do not figure in a report made in such desperate circumstances.

For further reading: Diane Purkis *The English Civil War* Harper Press, 2006.

FOUR

Along the Towpaths

Before the advent of the railways in the mid-nineteenth century, the transport of bulky materials such as coal, stone, grain and timber was undertaken by boats wherever navigation was possible. The buoyancy of a boat in the water enabled a heavy load to be moved with much less effort than that required to pull a laden wagon along rough roads.

On the river Severn, which gave the industrial Midlands a link with Bristol and the sea, transport was largely by Severn trows. Trows were flat-bottomed, wooden boats with a 'D' shaped cross section, and often had a square sail and a hinged mast which could be lowered to pass under bridges. Many were built locally. They were up to about 70ft long, 18ft wide and could carry more than 60 tons. They were well suited to the Severn, which is tidal to just upstream of Gloucester, and could withstand running aground on the sands and mud flats of the estuary. There are several rotting hulks of trows in the mud at Purton, near Sharpness, where they have been used to reinforce the river banks, and a rebuilt Severn trow, the Spry, is at Blist's Hill in the Ironbridge Museum.

The prevailing wind in the region of the Severn estuary is from the south west. Winds blow from this direction for about two thirds of the year. This south-westerly wind provided ideal motive power for ships coming up river, and the incoming tide assisted in their movement. The ebb tide and the normal flow of the river water helped with the return journey. Beyond the tidal limit and where the river was narrower, the energy to move the boats was provided by manpower when wind and river flow were insufficient. A scale model in the Ironbridge Museum shows trows being pulled in this way. A looped rope or bow from the top of the trow's mast was pulled by a team of men known as bow-hauliers, and by these the boats were moved up and down river. A rope coming from the mast in the centre of the boat, not only cleared river bank obstructions, but also helped in steering, because a rope attached to the bow would pull the boat towards the towing bank, while one from the stern would turn it towards the opposite bank. As many as fifty bowhauliers were sometimes required to pull a large ship against a strong river current, but old prints usually show a mere handful. And for bowhauling a towpath was required.

Bowhauling was a low-status occupation, and the men employed in this work were reputed to be typically dishonest and violent. They were gradually replaced by horses from the beginning of the nineteenth century - the horses using the same towpaths as the bowhauliers. For horses, the gates and stiles had to be removed and the towpath surface strengthened, and the first section of the Severn towpath to be improved in this way was from Ironbridge to Bewdley. This was opened in 1800. The horse towpath was later extended to Worcester in 1804, and to Gloucester in 1811. After 1860 steam tugs began to replace horses, and so the significance of the Severn towpath for the industry of the West Midlands declined from this time.

In the lower and tidal stretch of the river, navigation was always difficult. Frequent and unpredictable changes in the channel, strong tidal currents and seasonal variations in river discharge combined to cause these difficulties. The port of Gloucester could only be reached regularly with the monthly spring tides, and sea-going ships often travelled no further upstream than the small quays at Purton, Gatcombe and Newnham on the right bank of the river. But in 1793, following an earlier survey to assess its feasibility and when canal-building programmes were at their most popular in the country, an Act of Parliament was passed for a canal to be constructed from Gloucester to Berkeley. It was thought that such a canal would avoid the worst problems of the winding river. In the following year, after some limited capital had been raised, work began on digging the canal.

It was originally intended that the canal would be 70ft wide, 15ft deep and 18 miles long, but progress in digging the channel was slow. Costs rose steeply in the 1790s, and this increase, together with winter flooding and some management problems associated with excavating the canal basin at Gloucester, meant that by 1799 the canal had only reached

Hardwick, a distance of five miles, and the capital was exhausted. The low lying, flat land by the river has always been vulnerable to flooding, and the local geology of Lias clay contains within it bands of a harder Lias limestone, which are more difficult than clay to cut through. So delays in construction were almost inevitable. And today, when walking the towpath, it is noticeable that in some places nearer Gloucester the canal follows shallow cuttings through low hills, while at others it is many feet above the surrounding farmland. There are several long straight stretches to the canal, but the route finally chosen has a number of bends. These allowed canal digging to avoid the more expensive cuttings through the hills, as well as the more difficult stream crossings. There were also other obstacles to avoid such as the duck decoy pool on the Berkeley estate at Purton to placate a powerful landowner. The last stages of the canal's construction were overseen by Thomas Telford, and a shorter route leading to Sharpness rather than to Berkeley was chosen. It was finally opened in 1827, thirty-four years after the original Act of Parliament.

The entrance to the canal is by locks at both the Gloucester and Sharpness ends, where there are similar lock-keeper's houses, and there are also locks where it crosses the older and lower Stroudwater Navigation at Saul Junction. The towpath follows the western side of the canal all the way, for it is normal for a towpath to be on the 'downhill' side of a canal, so that the construction of the towpath can reinforce the canal bank. Originally, canal towpaths were not public rights of way, they were owned by the canal companies. And because this one was designed from its inception for use by horses, it was 7ft wide and constructed of stone brought from Bristol and surfaced with gravel from the gravel pits at Frampton. It is now maintained by British Waterways as a towpath trail, a leisure footpath, and parts of it also form sections of the National Cycle Trail 41.

Fifteen double swing bridges were built across the canal, where lanes gave access to farms and settlements nearer to the Severn. The bridges are named after nearby villages, farms or local landscape features. Each was worked from a bridge-keeper's house, or from a hut if the first bridge-keeper already had a house in the neighbourhood. Canal companies had their own distinctive designs for their houses, and in this case it was for small, single-storey cottages with white stucco walls, shallow slate roofs, and unusually large porticos with Doric columns. They were sited with

Splatt Bridge near Frampton church with a typical single-storey bridge-keeper's house.

good views up and down the canal and are on alternate sides. Once the canal was in use day and night, it was essential to have a keeper available at all times. The bridges at Hardwick and Pegthorne have now gone, but all eight bridge-keepers' houses have survived. Wind would have been a problem both for boat hauling and for the bridge-keepers and 'hobblers', when each side of the swing bridges was manually operated. Hobblers were men who walked the towpath, accompanying each boat. In addition to opening one side of each swing bridge, the other side being the responsibility of the bridge-keeper, they also used ropes to steady the boats when these approached constrictions on the canal and boats travelling in the opposite direction. Hobblers were replaced after the First World War by 'passmen', who cycled along the towpath rather than walking it, but performed the same functions. The mechanically operated single-span swing bridges were all introduced after 1950 and the latest is the hugely impressive Netheridge Bridge, which was completed in 2007.

Large, clearly visible, iron mile posts give the distances to Gloucester (G) and Sharpness (S). They are painted white with sunken black lettering. Numerous iron bollards also line the towpath, some are large and bulbous, most are shaped like the old-fashioned wooden clothes pegs used for peg dollies. No doubt passing the succession of mile posts gave

Gloucester Docks. The North Warehouse on the right has a builder's plaque beneath the eaves. It has been converted to offices for the City Council, while the Lock Warehouse is now an antiques centre.

much needed encouragement to the towpath users.

The landscape of the canal route is mainly of flat meadows, traditionally used for cattle grazing – originally for the Gloucester breed, which produced milk for the Double Gloucester cheeses, but now mainly for Friesians. On some better-drained land maize and potatoes are grown, and the low lying, wetter New Grounds near Slimbridge, where the corrugations of water meadow management still show, are used for the summer fattening of cattle and sheep. Most of the old brick-built farm houses are on slightly higher ground, and the succession of square towers of the village churches at Hardwick, Whitminster, Saul and Frampton catch the eye. The tall spire at Slimbridge is another notable landmark in the Vale. In the distance, the line of the Cotswold escarpment and the eastern rim of the Forest of Dean form the backdrops. Mature oak trees dot the adjoining fields and there has been some ornamental planting of cedars near the country houses. At Frampton two rare black poplar trees grow beside the raised bank of the canal and elsewhere pollarded willows are common. The latter gave some wind protection for canal users, otherwise it is an open landscape and often very exposed.

Beside the dock basins at Gloucester is the magnificent collection of warehouses. There are now fourteen of them, all are brick built and of a similar design, although their construction dates span nearly fifty years. The earliest is the North Warehouse, which was ready for the opening of the canal. It has four floors (most have five), each timber floor being supported by cast-iron columns. Hoists enabled sacks of corn to be lifted to each floor, where they were stacked in three tiers. The basements, which were secured behind iron-barred windows, were often used for the storage of wines. The North Warehouse has a stone plaque beneath the eaves giving the name of its builder, William Rees, and date, 1826. There is some slight variation between the warehouses in the size and shape of the windows and in the design of the roof eaves, but most are uniform. Their purpose was to store corn, which had been imported from different parts of Europe and brought in by sea-going ships, before it was transhipped up the Severn in long boats. Long boats were about the same length as Severn trows, but less than half their width, and carried about 30 tons. All the warehouses have now been converted to other uses and the dock basins are used for leisure craft. It must have been a great relief to the early hauliers and hobblers for the cathedral tower and then the warehouses to come into view, after their 16½-mile journey. The four warehouses at Sharpness were built to a similar design to those at Gloucester, but with six floors. Beside the locks of the Old Dock at Sharpness is a long low brick building. This was once the stables for the towpath horses. There were other stables at Saul Junction.

The vessels using the canal today are leisure boats. Many are long boats, colourfully decorated, with lettering showing their permanent mooring places – principally Gloucester, Saul, Frampton and Sharpness, but the names of Fretherne, Splatt Bridge and Slimbridge may also be seen painted on their sides. They are moored along the canal, usually near to bridge access points. Soon there will be additional mooring at the new marina at Saul Junction. The canal banks have been strengthened by steel piles to prevent damage by boat wash and choppy water, and at frequent intervals are the pegs for match angling. Swans and mallards, moorhens and coots, gulls and wagtails are commonly seen. There are usually several pairs of great crested grebes on the canal and in summer swallows drink from the water as they skim over the surface. Between September and March skeins of wild geese fly over the canal on the way to their winter grazing on the Dumbles at Slimbridge. It is a peaceful, colourful and varied environment, popular for towpath walking. But, as with all the canals, most walkers are unaware of the hard labour of those who first used the towpaths.

Although the Gloucester-Sharpness Canal was the most important canal in the area from a commercial point of view, there were earlier canals, and the Stroudwater Navigation and its extension as the Thames-Severn Canal were chief of these. The Stroudwater Navigation was opened in 1779. It was built so that coal could be carried from the Forest of Dean, and other more distant sources, to the woollen mills of the Stroud area. Coal was needed when steam power replaced the water power of the river Frome and its tributaries for driving the mill machinery. Coal from Forest of Dean mines was brought to the small right bank ports of the Severn on the backs of mules or by horse drawn wagons along poor roads. At these ports, and especially at Bullo Pill after the construction of its own tramway feeder line in 1809, coal was loaded on to Severn trows and these entered the Stroudwater Navigation at Framilode. Until 1827, when the Gloucester-Sharpness Canal was opened, the Stroudwater Navigation Company only allowed boats to be moved along their canal by bowhauliers or by the wind in their sails if conditions were favourable. At the time of planning the canal, neither donkeys nor horses pulled boats along the Severn, and so no provision was made for their use on the towpath here. The path was narrow, and where the canal cut across field boundaries, stiles and gates were erected along it. A very informative late eighteenth-century painting of Wallbridge, displayed in the Stroud Museum, shows the arrival of one such coal-carrying trow, with mast lowered to pass beneath the road bridge, and pulled by a bowhaulier. The tow rope in this case appears to be attached to the bow of the trow and is looped around the shoulders of the bowhaulier. It took a day for a trow to travel from Framilode to Stroud. Eventually six new woollen mills were built along the Stroudwater Navigation between Eastington and Ebley, demonstrating how significant this canal had become, not only for the transport of coal but also for wool and cloth.

The Thames-Severn Canal was a more imaginative venture. Although Lord Bathurst of Cirencester Park appreciated the significance of the canal and the Sapperton Tunnel to the landscaping of his estate, it was mainly promoted by interests outside Gloucestershire, as a means of transporting coal, iron products and other manufactured goods from the West Midlands to the lucrative London market, and also to link Bristol with London, when coastal trade between the two cities was insecure.

There was an urgency about its construction because other potentially competing canals were being planned at the time. From Wallbridge, the terminus of the Stroudwater Navigation, the chosen route followed the Frome valley upstream to Sapperton. Here, the highest part of the Cotswolds was tunnelled through. Then, after a further cutting, an abandoned valley of an earlier Thames tributary was followed. After winding north to Cirencester, the canal eventually joined the Thames at Inglesham. With its forty-four locks and a tunnel, which at 2.2 miles was the longest in the world, the twenty-nine miles long canal was a major engineering feat of its day. It took only five years to build, and its opening in 1789 warranted a royal visit. The western part of the canal as far as Brimscombe was wide enough for Severn trows but beyond this, and especially through the 15ft feet-wide tunnel, narrower Thames barges were required. So Brimscombe Port, with its excavated basin capable of holding 100 boats, was the transhipment point.

The responsibility for maintaining the canal and its towpath and of overseeing the locks was given to lengthmen. To house them the Thames-Severn Canal Company built twelve lengthmens' houses, five of which are distinguished by being round. Wharfs at convenient bridge points and several warehouses were also built, and the wharf houses still

A Thames-Severn Canal round house at Chalford.

survive at Stroud, Cricklade and Kempsford. Some of the houses and inns built along the canal were so isolated from the roads that normal social contact and business transactions would have only come from the canal users.

Despite its early promise the enterprise was never very profitable. It faced huge obstacles, some of which were unforseen. The maintenance of the tunnel proved costly; large volumes of water had to be pumped into the higher parts of the canal, particularly in summer when it was far above the water table; trade was significantly imbalanced, with 83 per cent going east; and stiff competition developed from other canals and then from the GWR. After a long struggle, notice was given in 1893 to close it east of Chalford. Local opposition influenced the Gloucestershire County Council to attempt to restore it, but this costly restoration work was never lasting, and following a gradual decline, the tunnel was closed in 1927, and the whole canal in 1933. The Stroudwater Navigation was more successful and its Act of Abandonment for Navigation was delayed until 1954.

Today, the towpath may be followed all the way from Eastington to Sapperton, and then in sections east of the tunnel. There was never a towpath through the tunnel, the boatmen had to leg it as they lay on planks. After 1827, following the opening of the Gloucester-Sharpness Canal, horses and donkeys were used on both canals. These had to walk over the tunnel, through the lanes and Hailey Wood, to either the classical style portal at Coates or its battlemented counterpart at Sapperton, where they joined the boat after it had been legged through the tunnel. One horse could pull a boat, laden with 60 tons of coal or stone, along the canal at about 2mph, but all the towing before 1827 was by bow hauliers, who earned from 10d to 1s 6d per ton of cargo. The journey to London took nine or ten days, and twelve to fourteen days were needed for the return journey, which was against the flow of the Thames. Physical strength and stamina were the main requirements for bow hauling and, although there was companionship on the journey, the work was hard and tedious. Brief rests from towing were possible as the boats passed through the locks, and canal-side inns were spaced at regular intervals. A few of the latter remain such as the Daneway and the Tunnel House at either end of the Sapperton tunnel, but most have gone or become private houses.

Industrial buildings of different dates line both canals from Stonehouse to Chalford. Some are stone built and were originally woollen mills as Ebley

Ebley Mill. The river Frome is to the left and the Stroudwater Canal to the right. In the distance is new canalside housing.

Whitehall Bridge with the towpath beneath. It is typically brick-built with some stone edging and the central stone is inscribed WD 1784.

Mill, Bourne Mill at Brimscombe, and St Mary's Mill and Belvedere Mill at Chalford; others are of brick, concrete and asbestos, in various states of repair, and with their strange assortment of chimneys and pipes. Occasionally round-headed or flat-topped milestones survive, usually without the iron plates, which once indicated the distances to Wallbridge and Inglesham. The distances were measured at ½-mileintervals from Wallbridge, which explains the ¼-mile and ¾-mile readings to Inglesham. Milestones were needed because the charges for the use of the canal were based both on the weight of goods transported and on the distance travelled. Stone edgings of the towpath still show where wharfs existed for unloading coal or mark the site of a former lock. Many elegant hump-back bridges cross the canals. These are brick built along the Stroudwater and mainly brick with stone coping on the Thames-Severn Canal. They carry the lanes and tracks which cross the valley floor. A few bridges have no space for the towpath to go under them, and here the tow rope had to be unhitched when passing them. Where a bridge is close to a bend in the canal, tow ropes have often cut deep grooves into its brickwork. At Chalford a small, well built, stone bridge bears the inscription 'CLOWS ENGINr 1785'. Josiah Clowes was the resident engineer for the canal construction. And near the Daneway, Whitehall Bridge has a stone inscribed WD 1784. This section of the canal was the responsibility of William Dennis. It has been suggested that subtle differences in the locks, wharfs and bridges along the canal reflect the piecework nature of the original building programme, but they may also result from the more than 100 years of subsequent repair work.

Beyond Chalford, the Golden Valley narrows. The untidy clusters of houses clinging to the hillsides and the tall mill buildings are left behind. Woods cover the steep slopes and meadows the valley floor, and apart from residents at the isolated houses, the only people seen are walkers following the towpath. The whole valley is important for the conservation of wild life. There is a notable display of lily-of-the-valley and its associated angular Solomon's seal in Siccaridge Wood near the Daneway, there are banks of primroses and bluebells in the spring and the scenery is enhanced by the lake at Baker's Mill. This former mill pond was enlarged by the canal company to provide a water supply for the locks. The quietness, without the noise of road traffic and of trains – apart from their distant whistles – is reminiscent of the canal age.

The canal may be followed for a short distance after the tunnel, but beyond Thames Head the towpath and often the canal itself disappear

Baker's Mill. The canal company enlarged the mill pond to supply water to the lock system.

until east of Cirencester. Now the canal crosses low-lying land, once mainly water meadows managed for hay crops, of which the Cricklade North Meadow, famous for its magnificent April display of snakeshead fritillaries, is a lone survivor. Much land has been lost to the extensive flooded gravel pits of the Cotswold Water Park. The towpath passes several of these lakes with their range of designated uses, and may be followed either side of the Gateway Centre. But there is at present little opportunity for towpath walking beyond the Basin near Cricklade, where the Thames-Severn Canal joined the North Wilts Canal. After Lechlade the Thames Path National Trail generally follows the old tow path.

The closure of the Thames-Severn Canal, once described as 'this most beautiful and most tragic canal', was regretted by many, and since the 1970s attempts have been made to restore parts of it. Temporary dams have enabled short sections to hold water, but where silt has accumulated, much of the channel has become filled with wetland vegetation – rushes, bulrushes, meadow sweet, comfrey, purple loosestrife, willow herb and occasionally yellow flag iris. The industrial sections of the canal, with their stagnant water, dank vegetation, ugly blockages and plastic rubbish, bordered by derelict or shoddy buildings, are not visually attrac-

Yellow flag iris brighten the silted canal bed in the spring.

A modern road bridge at the Cotswold Water Park Gateway with capacity for boats to pass beneath the bridge once the canal is restored. The steel railings represent bullrushes.

tive at present, although there are many features of industrial history to interest the walker. But change is imminent. With more substantial financial backing it is planned to restore both canals to full working order from Saul Junction to Brimscombe, and ultimately to Lechlade. Clearance work has started in a few places, some locks have been restored, and already new canal-side housing developments have begun. Major works were scheduled to begin in the autumn of 2007 and modern bridge building has been designed to allow for this canal reopening. One of the early objectives of the Cotswold Canal Trust, which has promoted the restoration programme, has been to encourage leisure walking along the towpath, as well as to allow for boating, fishing and the enjoyment of the wildlife along its course. Towpath restoration and reopening has already occurred in parts of the eastern section and more is anticipated soon.

Whether originally designed for horses and hobblers, as with the Gloucester-Sharpness Canal, or for bowhauliers along the Stroudwater and Thames-Severn Canals, the towpaths today make easy and interesting paths for ramblers. They are now public rights of way. They give access to the many natural and man-made landscape features that would have become very familiar to their earliest users, as they pulled their boats for mile after mile on their long journeys. Like the medieval salt ways and the eighteenth-century drovers' ways, towpaths had important roles in the early transport of essential commodities.

For further reading: David Viner *The Thames and Severn Canal* Tempus, 2002; Hugh Conway-Jones *The Gloucester-Sharpness Canal* Tempus, 2005.

FIVE

The Drovers' Ways

Over a period of several centuries, cattle, which had been reared in mid- and west Wales, were driven across the country to the markets and fairs of England. Here they were sold as store animals for fattening, to meet the beef requirements of the towns of the English Midlands and especially of London. As the city grew in the eighteenth and nineteenth centuries, so the opportunities for cattle droving steadily increased until the spread of the railways began to curtail this traffic. Some of the cattle destined for London passed through Gloucestershire on their way to the grazing pastures of the Thames Valley and the south east of England, and place names which include London are sometimes found along the old drovers' routes as in Little London at Longhope and at Lechlade.

The cattle moved at the slow, steady pace of about 2mph, occasionally feeding as they walked, and covered 15-20 miles a day. At night they rested in rented fields, while the drovers found accommodation in a wayside inn or farmhouse, or slept with the animals. These fields were sometimes named after the night's charge per head of cattle, as for example Halfpenny Piece, and the heavy manuring received from the resting cattle gave a welcome lushness to the grass of these fields that often distinguished them from neighbouring fields. It was conventional to plant Scots pine trees to indicate to the drovers where these resting places were to be found, but it is unlikely that the original trees have survived to the present day. Cattle required shoeing for the journey and so, for replacement shoes, blacksmiths' forges were sometimes found along the drovers' routes. Thus inn, rented field and smithy were clustered. This is well illustrated by the Five Mile House on Ermin Way, between Birdlip

Pevensey Levels in Sussex. One of the destinations for fattening Welsh cattle.

The Five Mile House on Ermin Way near Duntisbourne Abbots. This was a drovers' inn with a blacksmith's forge in the building on the left.

Welsh black cattle, small hardy animals.

and Cirencester, where the barn adjoining the inn was once a smithy. The cattle were mostly Welsh Blacks, small tough animals, three or four years old, which had been reared on the relatively poor grazing of the harsh environments of the mountain farms. Such animals were well able to make the journey, and had the advantage of putting on flesh quickly when provided with good grazing. They were bought by the cattle dealers and drovers at the Welsh fairs or directly from the farms, and often on credit.

A drove normally consisted of between 100–400 animals, divided into smaller batches, each of which was herded by three or four men and their dogs. Some drovers walked, some rode on horseback. From time to time, other travellers joined the drovers because, with the ever-present risk of robbery on the road, there was greater safety in numbers. The journey took three weeks to a month to complete, during which time the drovers were responsible for the welfare of the cattle. Because the cattle and the price they fetched at market represented the livelihood of the Welsh farmers, drovers had to be reliable and trustworthy men. Some were also entrusted to carry important letters and quite large sums of money. They were licensed, and this usually required them to be over thirty years old, married and householders. Many were chapel-going, and one at least, Dafydd Jones of Caeo near Llandovery, was sufficiently proficient in English to translate Isaac Watts' hymns into Welsh, having acquired the necessary language skills through years of cattle droving. Well-publicised court cases involving a few dishonest drovers tended to give the others a bad name. However, they may not have been so respected by the residents of the places they passed through. The huge numbers of animals would have obstructed other travellers, tracks would have been left in a filthy state, and it was often necessary to move the local cattle to the other side of the parish to prevent them from joining the drove. There was also the difficult problem of the supply of drinking water to so many animals. Drovers were relatively well paid and earned twice the wage of farm labourers. In addition to the sale money they carried back to Wales, they also brought back to their isolated mountain communities essential purchased goods and news of the outside world. They were capable of walking long distances and one is reputed to have won a £300 wager by walking 400 miles in six days. Drovers did not always return by the same routes as they took their cattle. The more wealthy sold their horses at the markets and fairs, and returned by stage coach. But it is said that their dogs found their own way back along the familiar routes, receiving food from the drovers' inns.

The routes they travelled were as direct as possible, while avoiding the main towns and the estates of the landed gentry. The rivers Wye and Severn were crossed by bridges, ferry boats or by swimming. At Tewkesbury after 1826, when the Mythe Bridge was opened, and also at Gloucester, bridges were used; at Aust, the ferry; and at Arlingham, the shallow river crossing. After the Parliamentary Enclosure Acts had fixed the field boundaries, and turnpiking had imposed charges on users of the main roads, the drovers' ways were more constrained. Fixed roadside boundaries such as walls and hedges eased the task of droving by channelling the cattle, but many drovers followed diversions to avoid the charges at the turnpike gates. Some tolls were inevitable, however, and the turnpike roads were usually the most direct routes. Typical toll gate charges were 10d for twenty cattle and 5d for twenty sheep, but the charges depended on the spacing of the toll gates.

The Welsh Way, which avoided Cirencester, is a typical drove road. It is marked on the Ordnance Survey maps as linking Ermin Way, the old Roman road at Middle Duntisbourne, to Fairford, a distance of about

The Welsh Way across the Cotswolds, a typical drovers' road. Notice the wide verges where hundreds of cattle could pass and feed as they walked.

A large field at Barnsley which was often rented by drovers from the Revd Charles Coxwell for the night's rest of their cattle.

eleven miles. Today, this is a lonely and bleak road, with very few houses, even at the crossroads, as it winds and zigzags across the Cotswolds. The country here is open, with distant views and broad skies. A 'Single Track Road' sign belies the wide space between the walls and hedges of its adjacent field boundaries. This width was characteristic of drove roads after enclosure, and was often twice that of other roads. Some of the wide verges have now been encroached upon by trees and shrubs, and not only by the hawthorn, blackthorn and elderberry of the enclosure hedgerows, but by field maple, hazel, oak and spindle. These clear indicators of old hedgerows on the Cotswolds hint that the borders of the Welsh Way may be much older than the dates of local Parliamentary Enclosure Act. In the autumn these hedges are festooned with the shining red berries of bryony and the silvery filaments of travellers' joy. The wide verges, which allowed the cattle to feed as they travelled, may sometimes have a distinct plant community, which was tolerant of grazing and manuring. Cow parsley, great knapweed and black horehound are typical verge plants. The verges of the Welsh Way have long been used as temporary sites for gypsy caravans, especially at the time of Stow Fair. At Barnsley, the only village passed on the Welsh Way, the route skirts the north end of the village, beside the boundary wall of Barnsley Park. The accounts of an eighteenth-century rector of Barnsley, the Revd Charles Coxwell, show an income of £1-10s for the use of the upper part of his 10-acre field by 100 cattle on 21 August 1779, and on October 23 of that year the lower part of the same field brought an income of £2-10s from Welsh cattle. On the 28 October 1782, £1-7s was received for the accommodation of fifty cattle on his 3-acre field, and on 6 November 1782, 12s for another small drove. Perhaps variations in the availability and the quality of grazing account for the differences in the charges. Most journeys were made either in the late spring or in the autumn. In the spring there was plenty of grass on the way, and the animals would have been fattened on high-quality grazing pastures at the end of their journey. The autumn droves, when food on the way was scarce and therefore more costly, led eventually to stall fattening on hay, straw and turnips. At this later time of year there was also the risk of damaging the soil structure of the fields by poaching, i.e. destroying the natural drainage of the field by trampling when the ground is too wet. The fields at Barnsley would have been vulnerable in this way, despite the partially improved drainage resulting from their shallow medieval ridges and furrows. After Fairford, the cattle moved on to Lechlade, then to Faringdon and Wantage, before climbing on to the Ridgeway, and so either on to Aylesbury for fattening or to fairs such as the great one at Barnet. It was at Smithfield that the highest prices were to be obtained for the fattened cattle. The drovers' inns along the Welsh Way were the Bear at Perrott's Brook, the Greyhound at Barnsley and the Ready Token Ash. The Greyhound was established here at Barnsley after the turnpiking of the Cirencester to Burford road in 1753. None of these are inns today. Before turnpiking had improved the roads that passed through the towns, the Welsh Way had been a main road, and it was referred to as the 'Gloster Road', i.e. London-Gloucester road, in Ogilby's *Britannia* of 1675, and shown as such on Isaac Taylor's map of Gloucestershire dated 1777. It may even have been the sixteenth-century 'Tames' path', and used by that family in their movements between their properties at Rendcomb and Fairford. The churches in both of these parishes were built from the wool wealth of the Tames.

Another drovers' way across the Cotswolds, which is still preserved in the present day landscape, bypassed Northleach. This was the route from Gloucester to London via Burford, Witney, and Oxford. The track left the turnpike road by the Puesdown Inn, another old drovers' inn, and rejoined it to the east of Northleach, thereby avoiding the toll gate near Hampnett. It was then known as the 'grene lane'. Tall beech hedges border this track today.

The account books of leading Welsh drovers, which give details of expenditure on lodgings for the drovers, grass for the cattle and toll-gate charges, enable the reconstruction of other journeys. One such route from Llandovery to Hitchin and Aylesbury involved paying tolls at the Mythe Bridge at Tewkesbury, Tewkesbury turnpike, Toddington turnpike and Moreton turnpike, and the expenses of both grass and drovers' lodgings at Tewkesbury, Moreton and the Rollrights. Another route was through Winchcombe, Northleach, Coln St Aldwyn and Lechlade, presumably following the Salt Way, and yet another followed Ermin Way through Cirencester to Cricklade, and so on to the Ridgeway. It was on this last road that William Cobbett, in his *Rural Rides* of 1821, records passing about 2,000 Welsh cattle on their way to fairs in Sussex. Cattle, after crossing the Severn by the Passage at Arlingham, moved along the hillside south of the Frome valley, through a resting place at Middle Yard, and then eastwards over the Nailsworth valley and so on to Minchinhampton Common and beyond.

Cattle were not the only type of farm livestock to be driven along the roads and tracks of the county. The great sheep fairs at Stow-on-the-Wold attracted flocks from all over the Cotswolds and from further afield, and there were other important livestock markets at Chipping Campden, Cirencester, Northleach, Tewkesbury and Tetbury, as well as the major market at Gloucester. Sheep also required resting places on their journeys and travelled 10-12 miles a day, but because there were more local markets for them they did not travel as far as the Welsh cattle. Forty to 70 miles was the typical radius of a sheep fair catchment area.

Stow fair was held twice a year, on the five days around May 1 (the Feast of St Philip and St James) and October 13 (the Feast of St Edward the Confessor). It was normal practice to hold fairs at the time of the patron saint's feast day, and sometimes it seems that the patron saint was selected from the date of the fair. The dates of Stow Fair were later changed to May 12 and October 24, with the change of calendar. Fairs took place when there was less urgent work on the farms.

It has long been recognised that the sites of the great fairs had several common location characteristics. They were often at parish boundaries, on high ground, at the intersection of green ways, and close to religious

The Market Square with its cross at Stow-on-the-Wold. The court house was where the shop on the left stands today.

shrines and prehistoric earthworks. Stow Fair possessed each of these location factors, apart from a shrine – although St Edward's Well, near the junction between the Fosse Way and the Burford road, was reputed to have healing qualities for eye troubles. The parish of Stow-on-the-Wold was taken out of a corner of Maugersbury parish, many roads and tracks converged on its elevated position, and just to the east of the Market Square was the site of an Iron Age hill fort. Fairs may have originated at those places where people had congregated from early times. At Stow-on-the-Wold, the original market area was in the triangle formed on the south side by part of the ancient east-west ridgeway, now Sheep Street, on the east side by the Salt Way running NW-SE, now the High Street, Market Square and Digbeth Street, and the Fosse Way on the west side. Within this triangular area the Market Square was eventually laid out with its adjoining burgage plots, which are still well preserved on the south side. Many markets originated in churchyards or even in the large church porches, but as they increased in size, land outside the churchyard was used, and then eventually the market squares or wide market streets were marked out. This may have been the case at Stow-on-the-Wold.

The charters for fairs and markets were granted by the crown, often as a favour for services rendered. Thus supporters of the king in time of war were often granted charters and so too were church authorities with the care of souls. The Stow market charter dates from 1107 and was granted to the Abbot of Evesham, who possessed the lordship of several manors in the area. The weekly Thursday market provided for the needs of the people living within a small radius. In the thirteenth century the appropriate catchment area for a market was judged to be one with a radius of 'six miles and a half and the third part of a half'. This distance was calculated by dividing twenty miles, the distance it was considered that people could conveniently walk in a day, into three. Theoretically one third of the day was spent walking to market, another third in market business and a third walking home. Neighbouring markets were held on different days of the week. This was so that packmen and pedlars could go from market to market with their goods, following a four or five day circuit. Thus Moreton market was on a Tuesday, Chipping Campden's on a Wednesday, Stow's on a Thursday, and Northleach market was on a Saturday or Wednesday. Traders followed this circuit along the roads and tracks that linked these market towns. Some of the market functions were later taken over by village shops, which began to appear in the early nineteenth century.

A narrow passage or 'ture' between the market and Sheep Street, Stow-on-the-Wold.

The charters for fairs at Stow were granted in 1330 and 1476, and in contrast to markets, the yearly fairs were on a much bigger scale and attracted traders not only from the local area, but also regionally, nationally and even from the continent. As well as business transactions, which at Stow included the sale of wool, hops and corn, fairs also provided entertainment for the visitors with wrestling and boxing, and news was shared. Fairs were big social occasions.

Shepherds drove their sheep to Stow along all the roads and tracks that converged on the hilltop. It has been suggested that the enclosure of the surrounding common fields contributed to the decline of the fairs by reducing the size of the sheep flocks, and the turnpiking of the roads would have increased the cost of conveying the sheep to and from the fairs. Apart from the turnpike gate near the Bell Inn on the Chipping Norton road, where the turnpike house still stands, the last turnpike gates before reaching Stow were all at the foot of the hill, at the bridges over the Evenlode and Dikler and at the last road junctions. Then the final climb began up to the site of the fair. Penned animals filled the Market Square and spread into Sheep Street. There is also documentary evidence of sheep being sold illegally outside the market area in the 1660s and again in 1816, thereby avoiding the market tolls. The Market Square was larger than it is today, and the central blocks of buildings, including St Edward's Hall and the shops beside the churchyard, are later encroachments. One building here, Cross House, by the market cross, stored the hurdles used in the market. Atkyns, followed by Defoe, records in 1712 that as many as 20,000 sheep were sold at Stow Fair, presumably over several days. The narrow winding alleys between high stone walls, known as 'tures', which lead from the Market Square to Sheep Street and to the Fosse Way and from Sheep Street to Back Lane, would have made it easier to count the animals as they entered or left the market. The ture, which leaves the Market Square to the left of the Talbot Inn, is little more than two feet wide in its narrowest place and this would have hardly allowed more than one sheep to pass at a time. The term 'ture' may have been derived from the French *tuyere*, and has also been applied locally to the narrow walled projections of Cotswold fields, which were designed to enable the cattle grazing in these fields to reach drinking water in the valley below. Four of these have recently been restored on the Stanway Estate.

The many visitors to the fair, who came from long distances, would have required nightly accommodation. This was usually provided by the historic inns of the town. There were inns in Sheep Street, as well as in the Market Square. Many have now become private houses or have been demolished, but a sufficient number remain as reminders of the scale of the fairs. They predate the coaching inns. The Talbot in the Market Square and the Unicorn in Sheep Street date from the early eighteenth century and were built on earlier inn sites, but the Swan (now Peppercorns) and the Crown (now Tudor House) in Sheep Street date from the fifteenth century. The King's Arms was established in 1548, and the White Hart and Queen's Head were first licenced in the seventeenth century. But there were many others, and it is recorded that in 1755 Stow-on-the-Wold had twenty-nine alehouse keepers.

It was also essential that any misdemeanour should be dealt with quickly, before the visitors left, so a court of pie powder was held. The name pie powder is corrupted from *pied poudre*, or 'dusty foot', and refers to the travelling pedlars that visited the fairs. The Court House stood on the corner where Church Street leaves the Market Square. Many market places had stone market crosses, symbolising the protection and security provided by the church, and where the market tolls were collected, and where the friars and others preached to the crowds. Public proclama-

Greenway Lane, Shurdington. An eighth-century sheep drove route linking two monastic estates.

tions were also made from the steps of the market cross, banns were read there and offenders were held up for public scrutiny. Stow's market cross dates from the fifteenth century, but its headstone is modern and the latest one depicts on its four sides four illustrations from the town's long history; a calvary, St Edward, the wool trade and the Civil War. The ringing of the church bells marked the beginning of the fair and there were processions and special church services held at the time of the fair. Stow market closed in about 1900, and by the end of the nineteenth century the fair had become a horse and pleasure fair. Today, Stow Fair is mainly associated with travellers and gypsies and the sale of horses.

With the recent closure of most livestock markets and the small abattoirs that served local areas, the long-distance transport of cattle and sheep is now by lorry. But until the 1950s, it was a common occurrence to encounter cattle and sheep driven along country roads and tracks to new grazing fields or to market. This local movement of livestock, which had continued for centuries, has also left its mark on the landscape. Thus drove roads, often green ways, linked the seasonal grazing areas of the larger estates. The summer grazing of sheep on the Cotswolds was followed by winter feeding and shelter in the farms at the foot of the escarpment. Sunken tracks, along which the sheep were driven, climb the scarp face in many places. Probably the best known is Greenway Lane, the lane beside the Greenway Hotel at Shurdington, which is thought to have linked land held at Badgeworth by St Peter's Abbey in Gloucester with its sheep-grazing pasture at Pinswell, near Upper Coberley. The Cotswold grazing land was acquired by the abbey in the eighth century. Running water from the numerous springs on the lower escarpment has contributed to the sunken nature of these tracks, but much mud would have been carried away on the hoofs of the animals driven along them. Similar tracks are to be seen at Kingswood, North Nibley, Stinchcombe and Leonard Stanley, and there are many along the edge of the north Cotswolds linking the lands of former monastic estates.

Thus radiating from the market places and medieval fairgrounds, linking seasonal grazing areas on the large country estates, and crossing the county from west to east and pointing towards London, are tracks, lanes and roads. For centuries, these have provided the routeways along which many thousands of cattle and sheep were slowly driven by farmers, shepherds and the more specialised drovers. Today, although some have become busy roads, many are quiet tracks where few people pass and where the vegetation beside the paths still reflects the long history of grazing and manuring by countless animals.

For further reading: Richard Moore-Colyer *Welsh Cattle Drovers* Landmark 2002.

SIX

Walking to Work

As long as rural labour was on a relatively small scale, workers tended to live on site, usually in free or rented accommodation. So on country estates and large farms employees often lived in tied cottages, fishermen along the Severn lived near their boat moorings, quarrymen close to the quarry and tradesmen at their work places. But as soon as rural work places began to employ more than a few people, the journey to work began to take on significance as a factor in the development of paths. By the early 1800s both coal and iron mines in the Forest of Dean employed more than 100 men in each of the main pits and the Stroud Valley woollen mills also employed more workers than could be housed in the immediate neighbourhood. Many of these late eighteenth- and early nineteenth-century industrial workers lived in squatter settlements, where the principal landowners had turned a blind eye on housing developments because they needed an enlarged work force for their industries. So on the upper slopes of the valleys of the river Frome and its tributaries, away from the mills, the power supplies and the transport routes in the valley floors, and on land that was on the edge of the commons, the cottages of spinners and weavers and other mill workers were spread out. Similarly, on the periphery of the Forest of Dean and sometimes within it, miners' houses sprang up on waste ground. To link these homes and workplaces many footpaths and tracks were made, and in some cases the actual site of the squatter's house was chosen because it was beside a suitable path to work.

Usually the shortest or easiest route was chosen to get to work quickly, and for the weary workers at the end of a shift it must have been some-

The Woolpack Inn, Slad.

thing of a relief to move into the open air along the footpath after long hours underground or bent over a loom. Unless the night was moonlit, the journeys to and from work in the winter months often took place in the darkness, before dawn and after dusk. To assist the spinners and weavers in finding their way across the commons at night, limewashed stones were placed beside the paths, and no doubt there was similar assistance for miners in the Forest of Dean. The daily walk to and from work gave much less variety of scenery than that experienced by the drovers, bow hauliers and pilgrims we have considered in earlier chapters, but could be just as unsafe, especially when wages were being carried home. And as with these other path users, horses, donkeys and mules sometimes assisted in the journey, often as pack animals. Donkeys were used for carrying woolpacks and cloth up and down the hillsides of the Stroud valleys and both donkeys and mules were used for transporting bags of coal and iron ore in the Forest of Dean, especially in the east of the area around Cinderford.

The rows of uniform terraced houses that were provided by entrepreneurs or by the mill and mine owners for their employees, were mainly built in the nineteenth century, and by this time work in the woollen industry and in mining was no longer a solitary or family affair. From then on, the social life associated with a populous work place was continued in such community activities as the brass band, choir, sports team and chapel life, and so other paths were formed to where these activities took place, as well as to the local inns. In this chapter we will consider the patterns of paths and tracks that were developed in both of these important areas of rural industry.

The floors of the valleys of the river Frome, Painswick stream and Nailsworth stream are narrow, shaded and damp. Wherever possible highly valued meadows occupied the bottoms, providing good quality grazing and hay. When water power was used to drive the mill machinery, the water courses were often artificially dammed, and a succession of mill ponds was formed to give a more reliable flow to the waterwheels of the mills. These ponds occupied other parts of the valley floors. The groups of mill buildings, which included stove houses where wool was dried after washing, dye houses and warehouses, as well as the fulling and gig mills and the first clothiers' houses, were beside the streams, and here was also some early densely packed housing. Consequently, with land along the valley floors already taken for meadow, pond and mill buildings, many spinners and weavers during the cottage industry period, and mill workers when spinning and weaving were mechanised processes using water power, had to live away from the valley floors.

The lower slopes of the valley sides are often very steep and wooded, and, since the woods were also a valuable resource, houses were not built here. The plateau surfaces above the valley sides were either the productive arable farmland of the common open fields or the old established farms, and so not available for buildings, or common land, protected from settlement because of their importance for grazing the sheep, donkeys and other animals belonging to all who had common rights. So the only suitable space for the squatter settlements was between the commons and the steeper slopes. Here arose the scattered weavers' settlements. They usually consisted of loosely formed clusters of eighteenth- and early nineteenth-century small stone cottages, some with mullion windows, arranged on terraces in a piecemeal way, and facing in different directions. As good light was needed for working at the looms, these were frequently placed in the attics, but if the looms were in a workshop or a room in the cottage, the windows of these rooms faced south wherever possible. The cottages had sloping gardens for home-grown

Former weavers' cottages scattered over Chalford Hill.

vegetables and fruit trees, a pig sty and a stable for the donkey. Hollows in the gardens frequently mark the places where the stone was quarried to build the cottages. Oakridge Lynch, France Lynch and Chalford Lynch (now Chalford Hill), above the Frome valley, and Watledge and Windsoredge above Nailsworth, are typical examples of these former weaver settlements, but there are many others. Samuel Rudder writing in his *New History of Gloucestershire* of 1779, describes how above Chalford 'the traveller sees houses intermixed with rows of tenters along the side of the hill on which the cloth is stretched in the process of making. In the bottom are eight fulling mills and in the villages above the hill called the Linchers a large number of people employed in the trade reside'. The word 'lynch' means a ridge or terrace, and the hillside here is known as Rack Hill, so called because the dyed cloth was hung out on the tenter hooks of racks to dry.

From the squatter settlements, footpaths and narrow lanes led down to the fulling mills. To these the cloth was taken to be pounded by the large water powered wooden hammers, known as stocks, in order to thicken it to a felt. There were fan-like patterns of paths converging on Baker's Mill and Puck Mill from Oakridge and Far Oakridge, and further west a more complex and dense network of paths and narrow lanes linked France Lynch and Chalford Lynch with the succession of mills at Chalford such as Ashmead's, Seville's, Halliday's, Bliss's, Randall's, Iles', Clayfield's and St Mary's. Some of the weavers' cottages were rented from the mill owners or from other weavers, and the weavers living in these cottages were more closely attached to particular mills and so used only one or two paths. But many of the squatters' cottages were held by the resident weavers themselves, and then the weaver could take on work from wherever he could get it, with a correspondingly more varied use of paths. In the latter case, cloth was sometimes carried long distances to a mill, perhaps even as far as Ebley or Cirencester. A characteristic desire for independence meant that many weavers were prepared to live well away from the mill, so as not to be under the eye of the clothier all the time. The large number of non-conformist chapels in the area also reflects this independence.

As is common with small lanes and paths almost everywhere, many were named after the people whose cottages bordered the paths. So we find various hills, lanes and pitches, as well as the mills themselves, named after families involved in the woollen industry. Today, many of the cottages have been gentrified with extensions, conservatories and landscaped gardens, and as they generally face south, they are in a pleas-ant suntrap. There has also been much infilling, so the gardens are not as large as formerly. Some cottages have names nostalgically associated with the woollen industry as Fleece Cottage, Weaver's Cottage and Teazle Cottage. The narrow roads, with their wayside wells and springs, are now mostly tarmaced. But the steep and stepped paths between stone walls, that linked the Lynches with the valley mills, remain little changed, though less frequently used than formerly. They form a key element of the old industrial landscape, and at Oakridge, the Oakridge Society has recently restored these paths because of their historical significance.

One of the early mill complexes, with many old buildings that have survived to the present day, is St Mary's Mill at Chalford. This mill origi-nally belonged to the church at Minchinhampton, and in 1600 had a dwelling, two fulling mills, one gig mill and a grist mill. The clothier's house on the east side of the yard still has a fine balustraded parapet and a shell hood over the central doorway on the south front. The architecture of the house demonstrates the growing prosperity of the clothiers in the eighteenth century. A narrow, four-storey stone mill opposite, with

The plaque recording the restoration of weavers' paths at Oakridge.

St Mary's Mill, Chalford, with the clothier's house in front.

pairs of windows to give good natural light, was built in about 1820. Its two waterwheels, which drove the machinery, were below the building where the water still flows. The tall brick chimney in an adjacent building is a reminder that, after the Thames-Severn Canal had been opened, coal could be brought in for producing steam to power the machines. Here, incorporated into the group of buildings, are structural features dating from the sixteenth to the nineteenth centuries. The nearest hillside settlement, from which weavers could come, was Brownshill.

The early industry was organised so that the clothier supplied the wool that was to be spun. It was collected from the mill and taken up to the cottages, where the women and children worked their spinning wheels. The skeins of spun wool were then returned to the mill, from which they were later redistributed to the weavers. Two men worked each broadloom in the weavers' cottages, and after two or three weeks' work of fifteen hours a day, the standard fifty-four yard lengths of cloth would be completed and returned to the mill for fulling and dyeing. At this time there was a regular movement up and down the hillside between cottage and mill. But once the whole process of cloth manufacture, including the spinning and the weaving, was at the integrated mill, the journeys to and from the mill for work took place on a more frequent daily basis.

The integrated mills in this part of the Frome valley ceased woollen production before the end of the nineteenth century. The high cost of coal, relative to that for the competing Yorkshire woollen mills, made them uneconomic. Some were demolished, others were adapted to new uses, and St Mary's Mill, Iles' Mill and Bliss's Mill became, for a time, centres for the manufacture of umbrellas and walking sticks. But by now the employees were no longer drawn solely from nearby weavers' cottages.

Turning now to the Forest of Dean, we find that Sir Robert Atkyns famously described how, just before 1712, when his *Ancient and Present State of Glostershire* was published, about 400 hovels of Forest dwellers, 'cabins of beggarly people', were cleared to leave only the original six keepers' lodges. Free miners, who for centuries had extracted the iron ore and coal for which the Forest was important, had to be born within St Briavels Hundred in order to qualify for mining rights. The majority of these free miners would have lived in the peripheral villages of the Forest, where Norman churches at Staunton, Ruardean, Hewelsfield and St Briavels, and thirteenth- and fourteenth-century churches at Littledean, Mitcheldean and Newland, indicate older settlements. The

scale of mining was small, and the shallow pits were quickly exhausted
or restricted by flooding and were consequently short lived. Miners
would then move on to another gale. A gale was a small area of land
with mining rights and was allocated by the gaveller, the Crown offi-
cial who was responsible for mining control. Because the mines were
only worked for a short time, to live close to a particular mine would
have been of limited advantage. The geological structure of the Forest of
Dean is a synclinal basin, and the seams of coal and the strata containing iron ore rise to outcrops around the edges of the basin. It was here,
therefore, that mining began and a peripheral settlement pattern was
convenient for the free miners. As the demand for coal and iron ore
increased, many more miners had to be employed, with a corresponding
expansion of the Forest population. The Revd H.G. Nicholls reports in
his book *The Forest of Dean, an Historical and Descriptive Account* that there
were 696 houses in the Forest in 1803 and 662 free miners. The population continued to rise rapidly reaching 5,525 in 1821 and 13,252 in 1851.
About half of the working population was employed in coal mining and
a quarter in the iron industry, when Nicholls wrote his book in 1858.
The later mines were deeper and more central to the Forest and each
employed several hundred miners, so for them new squatter settlements

Ruardean Hill, a former squatters' settlement for Forest miners.

The Trafalgar mine at work. It closed in 1925.

arose within the Forest. A good example of a former scattered mining settlement, with houses orientated in different directions and consisting of a succession of encroachments, is Ruardean Hill from which, in later years, miners travelled to the Northern United and Trafalgar collieries amongst others. Generally from the 1930s, miners were bussed to and from work, but before this they walked.

Large-scale coal mining finally ceased in the Forest of Dean in 1965, although a handful of drift mines worked by free miners has continued to the present day. From the numerous and widespread small pits, the industry in the nineteenth century was gradually concentrated on fewer but much larger ones. A typical example was the Trafalgar mine in the north central area of the Forest. The gale here was granted to Cornelius Brain of Mitcheldean in 1842, and mining began in 1860. Trafalgar rapidly became one of the leading collieries and at its peak employed 900 men. It was producing 500 tons of coal a day in 1906 and was still employing 360 miners in 1922. But by this time costs of production were rising, supplies of household coal were running out and there was unrest among the miners, and so the mines in this area of the Forest began to close one by one. Trafalgar ceased production in 1925.

The line of Brain's tramway along which Bill Williams walked to work.

The site of the Trafalgar mine in 2007. The stones mark the mine shafts in the 1870s.

A recently designated long-distance footpath, the Wysis Way, passes the site of this mine, and in such an isolated location one wonders where so many miners came from. There is a small nearby settlement at Brierley, and Cinderford is just over two miles away. But there were other large coal mines nearer to Cinderford than Trafalgar and these would have been more accessible to miners living in this Victorian mining town, and the iron mines on Edge Hills and the iron works in the valley bottom below Cinderford would have also attracted a workforce. So Trafalgar and other similar mines would have had to draw on a wider catchment area for its workers. One young mine worker who made the daily walk to Trafalgar was Bill Williams, a mine store keeper and clerk from Littledean Woodside. He tells us in his diary for 1872/73 that he had to be at work at 6 a.m., although he did not always make it by the whistle and then usually found a kindly reprimand for his late arrival chalked on his door by the colliery owner, W.B. Brain, son of Cornelius! He normally finished at 5 p.m., but twice a week worked on to midnight for additional income. The miners at Trafalgar worked in two shifts, from 6 a.m. to 2 p.m. and from 4 p.m. to 12 midnight. For part of the walk to work Williams would have followed the line of Brain's tramway. This was an early plateway linking Trafalgar with Drybrook and terminating near Euroclydon, the house built in about 1860 as the home for the original colliery owner's other son, T.B. Brain. From the tall square tower of Euroclydon it is said that the winding gear of Trafalgar could be seen. The tramway was constructed for transporting coal by horse- drawn trucks. It was later replaced by a railway on which a small tank locomotive pulled twenty to twenty five coal trams to Bilson, where the coal was loaded on to the trucks of the GWR. It took Williams about an hour to walk to work but he could run the distance in about twenty minutes, and in winter he often arrived at work cold and wet through. However, when he worked late, he usually got a lift home on a railway truck and then travelled more rapidly 'like lightning' or 'like wild fire', covering the mile and a half to Bilson in four minutes.

Today, apart from Trafalgar House, the former home of W.B. Brain, and a few stone walls of the remaining mine buildings, there is little to indicate the high level of activity once carried out here. Single standing stones mark the sites of the two 200ft deep mine shafts, and a nearby cone-shaped wooded hill is the former waste tip. On a summer day with the bright green foliage of the surrounding woodland and abundant bird song, it is easy to forget those who in all weathers, and often in the dark-

The weavers' path between Bradley Green and Wotton-under-Edge.

ness, trudged to work here for low wages and dangerous, back-breaking labour. And all this at the same time as A.O. Cooke was enjoying his leisure walks in the area, walks we will consider in a later chapter.

And so, just as paths converged on the woollen mills of the Cotswold valleys, they also converged on the coal and iron mines of the Forest of Dean. The former have been preserved in the landscape, but the removal, by the Forestry Commission, of most traces of mining in the Forest of Dean for safety reasons, and the replanting of the woodland, have obliterated many of the old miners' paths.

For further reading: Bill Williams *The Diary of a Working Man 1872-1873* Sutton 1994.

SEVEN

Promenading in Regency Cheltenham

The paths we have considered previously have all been associated with the essential movement of workers or goods and with religious and military travel. Now we will discuss the paths developed for leisure use.

Before the legendary observation of pigeons pecking at salt deposits by a spring, where the water did not freeze in hard wintry weather, Cheltenham was a small market town possessing a single long winding street and the few market structures of market cross, market house and booth hall. The parish church was set back from this street and there was also a grammar school and a 'great' house. Most buildings were of brick and Thomas Robins' painting of a view of Cheltenham from the west in 1748, now in the Cheltenham Museum, clearly portrays the red-brick colour of the town.

The owner of the farmland where the spring water seeped out was William Mason, and he was responsible for sinking a well here and enclosing it. The medicinal value of drinking mineral waters had long been recognised. By 1740 228 'spaws' had been established in England and the towns of Epsom, Tunbridge Wells and Bath had already capitalised on the fashion of 'taking the waters'. So Mason began to sell bottles of water from his own well, and to do so, not only locally, but also at more distant places including Bristol and London. This Cheltenham water was claimed to be 'a sovereign remedy in all hypochondriacal and bilious disorders, and an excellent stomachic tonic'. The recommended dose was for two glasses to be drunk, with a fifteen minute interval between them. However, Defoe had shrewdly observed that more was involved in drinking the waters at the early spa towns than the medicinal interest. He wrote in 1724, 'the coming to the wells to drink the waters was a mere matter of custom; some drink, more do not, and few drink physically. But company and diversion is, in short, the main business of the place'.

On Mason's death, part of his estate was inherited by his daughter, Elizabeth, who had married Captain Henry Skillicorne, and to Skillicorne Cheltenham owes its initial development as a spa town. As his unusually long epitaph in the parish church informs us, Skillicorne was a man of initiative and vision. He promptly deepened the well, and built over it an arched cover with a central finial in the roof, shaped like a lantern. On each of the pillars near the corners of this brick structure was a symbolic pigeon resting on an urn. Beside the well he also built a small ballroom, with billiard room above, and at a later date, on the opposite side of the well, the Long Room was added for parties and balls. The appearance of this group of buildings is recorded in a painting dated 1813, now also in the Cheltenham Museum.

To reach the well from the churchyard, which was the nearest access point from the single market street, Skillicorne laid out the Well Walk. This was a straight path, about 20ft wide, between a double row of

Cheltenham Museum has a display of nineteenth-century china portraying the Pump Rooms and the walks to the spas.

evenly spaced elm trees. Visitors could walk across the church meadow by a winding gravel path, cross the river Chelt by a rustic bridge or, as some reports state, a small drawbridge, and enter the Well Walk through an iron gateway. Beyond the well, the walk continued up the gentle rise and here it was bordered by elm and lime trees, with an adjacent orchard. The planting of the 133 trees beside the Walk took place in the winter months of 1739 and 1740, but in both the following summers the weather was very dry and many trees died. The Robins' painting, shows them as tall, spindly specimens. The dead trees were quickly replaced, and by the time of the 1813 painting, they had created a shady avenue in which to walk. In 1845, with the interlacing branches overhead, the walk was compared to a cathedral aisle. Long avenues of trees were then in fashion for landscaping the grounds of country estates, and the vista along this avenue, with the church spire and backdrop of Cleeve Hill at one end and the picturesque Grove Cottage at the other, was described as one of the noblest of its kind in England. Prestige was given to visits to the well by the 1740 publication of a report on mineral waters, which drew attention to the superiority of Cheltenham water, and by the highly publicised visit of George III in 1788. Ruff's *Beauties of Cheltenham* 1806 describes the view of the grand walk on a summer morning as one of the most interesting pictures imaginable 'whether is considered, the overflowing company, composed of the first characters of the kingdom – the distant harmony of the instruments – the fragrance of the air – or the circumstance, that is here combined, in the greatest possible degree, luxuriance of health, with the fascinating enjoyments of high life'.

Skillicorne had charged a shilling for entry into the Well Walk, which was later increased to 3s 6d, and he recorded the numbers of subscribers each year. His epitaph describes how he 'ever presiding with esteem in the walk, saw it visited with benefit by the greatest persons of the age'. It was a socially exclusive and financially profitable enterprise. A fuller description of life at the now 'Royal Well' was given in Ruff's *History of Cheltenham* 1803:

> The Spa Room is opened every morning for the accommodation of visitors. The sun has no sooner begun to absorb the cool dews of the morning, and the whole sky to be animated with its warmth and influence - no sooner has the lark ceased his first morning carol, and the general choir

of birds succeeded, than the busy hum commences at the well. Between six and seven the walks begin to be filled. From seven till nine they are crowded. Here may be seen a galaxy of beauty, which over-powers even Aurora herself. Here, the sparkling eye - the bewitching mein - the elegant costume, which fascinated all beholders at the evening ball - assumes an altered character. The warm glow of the midnight dance is exchanged for the fresh tint of the morning. The brilliant robe, the necklace, the ear drop, and the head dress, are transformed into an easier, a simpler, and, perhaps, more becoming attire.

This description is quoted in subsequent guides to Cheltenham, including Rowe's *Illustrated Cheltenham Guide* of 1845, and evidently still applied in the mid-nineteenth century, although by then, several other competing wells had been developed and the spa towns had been replaced by seaside and continental resorts as recreation places for the leisured classes.

Today, little remains of the Well Walk. The river Chelt passes underground in a culvert, St Georges Road and a car park cover the former entrance and parts of the lower walk, and the Cheltenham Ladies College has been extended over the site of the well – perhaps symbolic of Cheltenham's changed function in the second half of the nineteenth century from a spa town to an education centre. Church meadow, once used for cattle grazing, is now partly occupied by Royal Crescent, the first of the Regency housing developments. Royal Crescent originally overlooked the path to Well Walk in its view of the distant Cotswolds, but now faces the coach station and the ugly rear of the municipal offices. The small pedestrian way into the churchyard preserves the name Well Walk, and the wrought-iron gate piers at the entrance to the Walk have been removed and re-erected in the lane leading to The Crippets above Shurdington – although these were not the original ones and are not shown in the early prints.

The numbers of visitors to the well grew from just over 400 in the first year to more than 2,000 in 1800, and there was then insufficient mineral water to meet the demand. So more than 100 exploratory borings were made in other places on the south side of the small town. In 1801, a London financier, Henry Thompson, bought a large piece of land in this area and continued the search, sinking more than eighty wells. Different wells produced mineral water of varied salt content, and the clusters of physicians attracted to Cheltenham were later able to advise on the appropriateness of particular wells for specific ailments. Magnesium and sodium sulphates and sodium chloride were the main salts found in the underlying Lias clay, and the original analysis of the Cheltenham waters described them as 'purging chalybeate'. The practice of dieting, exercise and drinking spa water, together with promenading and resting, contributed to the leisurely pace of life associated with the town in the 1820s and 1830s, though humorous cartoons of the time painted a different picture of the effects of the waters. Thompson's successes in well borings led to the sale of water from a new site, Hygeia House, now Vittoria House in Vittoria Walk, which he had built as his own residence in 1804. To further capitalise on the potential of the area, he then built a new pump room at Montpellier, where Lloyd's Bank is situated today. Old prints show that this was a spreading pavilion-like wooden structure, with a veranda on at least three sides, and above the arched entrance was a balcony where a small orchestra played. The enclosed tree-lined walk sloped away towards the town on the north side, ending close to the upper part of Skillicorne's Well Walk. In front of the pump room, known originally as Thompson's Spa, he laid out Montpellier Gardens. Promenaders used these gardens in summer, and the walks there led to a

Montpellier Pump Room, Cheltenham.

band stand, pagoda and a very ornate marble fountain.

In 1817 the wooden pump room was replaced by the present stone building. Its architect was G.A. Underwood. It has an eleven-bay colonade on the east side, with Doric columns, stone urns on the corners of the parapet and a central lion couchant. To this substantial long low building was added, in 1826, the splendid copper dome and lantern that has made today's Rotunda. The architect for this addition was J.B. Papworth, who was employed by Thompson's son, Pearson, and was influential in the early development of the Montpellier and Lansdown estates. The spacious interior of the Pump Room, its design-based on the Pantheon in Rome, with its mirrors and central chandelier, its decorative urns and floral arrangements, its Corinthian pilasters and shafts of sunlight, enhanced the experience of those taking the waters. And to this Rowe adds his own appreciation of the Montpellier Walk – 'this beautiful walk, when crowded by its elegant and fashionable promenaders, and enlivened by the performance of the fine band of the establishment, conveys a pleasurable sensation of no ordinary kind'. The band then sat under the north side of the colonade, facing the walk. During the mornings 'the lovely, the titled and the fashionable' paraded along the walk to the sound of music. Musical promenades were held on three or four evenings a week during the season. The band of seventeen musicians began to play at 7 p.m. or 7.30 p.m. as the marble notice now in the Cheltenham Museum states, and the gardens and walk, which was then lined with seats, were lit with gas lighting. Gas lights replaced oil lamps in 1818. Once again, access was exclusive and by subscription only. The rules required that 'no servant of any description is allowed to come on the walk during the hours of the Promenade, or into the gardens at any time'. The gardens and walk were more elevated than the other spa walks and were characterised by 'pure refreshing air yet with shelter by the trees from the oppressive heat of the sun'. At the time of writing, work is under way to restore these gardens.

The west side of the original Montpellier Walk is now built over. Montpellier Arcade at its north end is dated 1831–32, and the bow-fronted building forming the entrance to the walk was added in 1843. The row of shops beside the walk, with their conspicuous caryatids, was built between 1843 and 1860, not in 1836 as the stone above the level of the balustrade at No. 26 indicates. There were a few small shops by the pump room before the present row was built and the earlier date may apply to these. Most of the caryatids were sculptured from stone in a Tivoli Street workshop and are copies of the original three white-painted Coade stone specimens, made for the entrance to the walk by the London sculptor, J.C.F. Rossi. They support an oak-leaf frieze. Nowadays, congested car parking in the road rather destroys the classical setting of this elegant walk.

In 1818 the Harward brothers, who owned land north of the Montpellier estate, began the layout of the next spa. This was the Sherborne Spa, named after the lord of the manor. For the spa building, they also employed G.A. Underwood as architect, and here the portico had six Ionic columns and above it, on a pedestal, was a figure of Hygeia. The building was placed in wooded surroundings, with gardens and a fountain in front. The gardens, originally referred to as botanic gardens and managed as Ware's nursery, with their cottage, green houses and hot houses, later became Imperial Gardens. Also of great importance for modern Cheltenham was the Sherborne Walk. This became the Promenade. It began at the Colonnade, the short street off the High Street, and extended for a quarter mile to the spa. There was a central carriage road and on either side a gravel walk. It was, as usual, tree-lined with a variety of trees including beech, sycamore, larch, pine, birch, elm and mountain ash, and the gardens in front of the spa, with their flowers and fruit trees, were again for the exclusive use of subscribers. The former swampy lane from the High Street, which led to a wooden plank over the River Chelt and marshy ground with stagnant water on the other side, was completely transformed. Contemporary guide books mention that all three spa walks were noted for their extensive views over the town to the surrounding hills, and they encouraged visitors to make excursions into the countryside around.

The speculative development of Cheltenham, which capitalised on its now abundant medicinal water, was handicapped by insufficient accommodation for visitors. This problem was tackled in two ways – by building houses that would attract wealthy and discriminating residents, persons of 'station, affluence and respectability', and by providing new hotels. The Promenade displays both solutions. The Imperial Hotel, now Waterstone's bookshop, was built in 1823 and the Queen's Hotel followed in 1837-38 on the site of the Sherborne Spa. The redundant latter building was dismantled and moved further down the Promenade to a site just behind the present fountains, and used here as a furniture

Montpellier Walk. Once an exclusive tree-lined walk.

Imperial Gardens, formerly the gardens for the Sherborne Spa which was on the site of the Queen's Hotel to the left.

1 Hawling wall with a distant tumulus covered by pink rosebay willowherb in the field opposite, as indicated in the charter.

2 The tomb of King Edward II, Gloucester Cathedral, a popular medieval shrine.

Opposite: 3 Gloucester Cathedral from the east. The perpendicular style of the south transept, choir and presbytery date from the mid-fourteenth century, and were partly funded by the gifts of pilgrims.

Right: 4 Sudeley Castle. Beyond the knot garden a wall still shows the damage caused by the slighting of the castle in 1649.

Below: 5 The site of the Battle of Stow, 1646. The monument commemorating the battle has been recently erected.

6 Saul Junction. The Gloucester–Sharpness Canal is at a higher level than the Stroudwater Canal, which is just beyond the boatyard crane.

7 Two bow hauliers pull a canal boat towards the Sapperton Tunnel 1793. (The Waterways Archive, Gloucester)

Above: 8 Another stretch of the Welsh Way where trees and shrubs have now colonised the grass verges.

Right: 9 St Mary's Church, Cheltenham. The lengthy epitaph to Capt. Henry Skillicorne can be seen inside.

10 'The effects of the Cheltenham waters' – an early nineteenth-century cartoon. (Cheltenham Museum)

11 Pittville Pump Room, completed in 1830.

12 Yew trees on the raised walkways at Cassey Compton in 2007.

13 Stanton with its village cross.

14 Broadway Tower, a folly built in 1800.

15 The old road to the deserted village of Pinnock.

Promenade Terrace, Cheltenham. A row of eleven houses built in the early 1830s.

The Colonnade joins the Promenade here. Jones' shoe shop was Wight's Theological Library in 1850, Martins' shop on the left has continued as a goldsmith and silversmith shop from the beginnings of Regency Cheltenham.

warehouse and showroom. New housing began with the very impressive long terrace, originally known as Harward's Buildings, and now forming the Municipal Offices. This effectively blocked the view of the Cotswolds from the Royal Crescent, as so frequently happened with independent housing developments. These houses were also designed by G.A. Underwood and built between 1822 and 1835, their private gardens with iron railings extending to the walks. The 1830s also witnessed the building of other houses on both sides of the Promenade, some were semi-detached villas such as Clarence House near the Queen's Hotel, others were short terraces. The eleven houses of Promenade Terrace is a good example of the latter. The detached houses on the east side of the Promenade are now masked by twentieth-century shop fronts and infill, and are best appreciated when viewed from the opposite side of the road. By the time of Rowe's *Illustrated Cheltenham Guide* of 1845, these houses had already become shops, although the ground-floor frontages were not as they are today. The merchandise sold in them reflected the expensive tastes of a wealthy clientele and in many cases those of retired East India Company officials and service officers, who had moved to the town. Only Martins' jewellers and watchmakers shop still remains from that 1845 survey of shop owners. The first department store, known from early days as Cavendish House, opened in 1826 as Clark and Debenham's, later to be Debenham, Pooley and Smith's. All the houses were built of brick, mostly of bricks made on site using the underlying clay, and with a stone or stucco facing. Their wrought-iron balconies and canopies with various delicate designs are still distinguishing features of Regency Cheltenham, as are their classical-style pillars and pilasters. The whole range of classical columns – Corinthian, Doric, Ionic and Tuscan – may be seen, no doubt prompted by the Grecian architecture of the spa buildings. The balconies of Imperial Square and of a number of other Regency terraces have the double heart design of their iron work. This standardised iron work was brought from Scotland, but in the Promenade the design of the iron work is different for each block of buildings. The houses were evidently built for gracious living, though their typically cluttered and untidy rear elevations were given much less attention than their frontages. The central location and pleasant setting of these houses has made them sought after for modern commercial and office use, and the consequent injection of capital has assisted in their excellent state of preservation. Regency property further out from the centre did not fare so well.

The tree-lined Promenade, looking north from near the Queen's Hotel.

The three rows of trees of the Sherborne Walk have been retained, although the predominant species have changed. Horse chestnuts replaced the original plantings and now plane trees are more common. The tapering width of the Promenade from the Queen's Hotel northward, which gives a sense of greater distance to this view and a sense of intimacy to the opposite view and applies both to the width of the road and the alignment of the buildings, is a feature original to the layout. Because the Promenade was planned as a spa walk and not a through road, the important new road from Cheltenham to Painswick and Bath went along what became the Royal Crescent, Montpellier Street, Lypiatt Road and Painswick Road and was turnpiked in 1819, with the first turnpike gate at the junction of Painswick Road and Shurdington Road.

By the time of the development of the Pittville Estate, at a discrete distance on the north side of the town, and the completion of its Pump Room in 1830, the enthusiasm for drinking mineral water and for elegant promenading was in decline, and the planning emphasis here was for a garden suburb. The landscaping of gardens had entered a new phase and the avenue or long walk was no longer in fashion. The rising lawn from the lake to the Pump Room was the promenade here. The Revd Francis Witts, rector of Upper Slaughter, who was fascinated by the early nineteenth-century growth of Cheltenham, records in his diary for 15 October 1833:

> Walked to Pittville, where we were, as non-subscribers, admitted on the payment of one shilling. The place is very well kept, the walks in excellent order and the shrubberies very much grown, and all the gardens very luxuriant. Though but a few individuals were in the splendid Pumproom, a small band of musicians, playing on wind instruments, performed many pleasing pieces of music.

Witts' visit was late in the season, which by now extended from May to October. At Pittville subscribers paid 5s for a fortnight's access to the walks and 15s for the year. For the Sherborne Walk, the seasonal charge was 3s 6d. The charge for drinking the water was in addition to this. A fortnight's drinking cost 10s 6d and for a full course of the waters the charge was a guinea. This too contributed to the exclusiveness of the spas for a labourer's wage at the time was about 1s a day.

Not all visitors to Cheltenham, however, were so impressed with the social life centred on the walks and pump rooms. William Cobbett's hostile comment in his *Rural Rides* of 1826 was perhaps extreme and provocative. He wrote:

> To places such as this come all that is knavish and all that is foolish and all that is base; gamesters, pickpockets, and harlots; young wife hunters in search of rich and ugly and old women, and young husband hunters in search of rich and wrinkled or half-rotten men.. a place to which East India plunderers, West India floggers, English tax-gorgers, together with gluttons, drunkards and debauchees of all descriptions, female as well as male, resort at the suggestion of silently laughing quacks in the hope of getting rid of the bodily consequences of their maniford sins and iniquities.

No wonder Cobbett was not welcomed in Cheltenham after the publication of *Rural Rides*!

There were other spas in Cheltenham, but these four had the biggest impact on the town's development and have contributed most to its spacious layout and tree-lined streets. Because they were developed independently, the resulting plan of the town centre is less coherent than that of most other nineteenth-century towns and has led to great difficulties in coping with modern through traffic, but it preserves a framework in which it is easy to picture the elegance of the early promenaders.

Attempts were also made to establish spas in other places within the county. Gloucester and Lower Swell still have evidence of spa buildings but nothing compares with the scale of development that occurred in Cheltenham in the early nineteenth century.

EIGHT

Up the Garden Path

In this chapter we will look at the development of paths within the ornamental grounds of the country houses of the county, paths which have had a variety of functions. But we begin with some medieval gardens. There were gardens in the grounds of the Benedictine monasteries in the towns, for example in Gloucester there was an infirmary garden attached to St Peter's Abbey, now the Cathedral. The Franciscans also had an important orchard in the city and the name Friars' Orchard is still used today. But of wider interest for early gardens are the Cistercian monasteries. Cistercian monks regarded their monasteries as symbolic of Jerusalem and thought of them as places of great spiritual beauty. Within their grounds specific places were linked to particular biblical sites, and to these the monks would go to meditate on the events recorded in the gospels at those locations. These meditations were partly undertaken in order to better prepare the monks for the heavenly Jerusalem. The paths to those places were also given special meaning. So at the Cistercian abbeys of Flaxley, Hailes and Kingswood, paths were for meditation, rather like the recent development of labyrinths such as we find by the small Norman church at Hailes or at the Matara garden at Kingscote.

Of early gardens in the county that have in part survived to the present day, the one at Thornbury Castle is of national importance. Here, in the decade from 1511, Edward Stafford, Duke of Buckingham, built his castle-palace and laid out his 'privie' and 'goodly' gardens and orchard. Contemporary documents tell that the latter was surrounded by a raised and covered alley, over which branches of whitethorn, crab apples, roses and hazel had been trained. Here, the duke could take his exercise walks

beneath the shade of the trees and in privacy, and could view the surrounding countryside from raised turf seats. The survey, made in 1521,
also mentions its notable knot garden of lavender and rosemary, designed
presumably to represent the Stafford emblem. During the summer
months this garden would have brought a fragrant scent to life within its
embattled walls. The main purpose of the garden walks, however, was for
physical exercise and this was also true of the shaded alleys of the gardens
of the next century.

We have to wait until Sir Robert Atkyns' *The Ancient and Present State
of Glostershire* was published in 1712, to find the first collection of illustrations of the county's gardens. Johannes Kip's engravings of the seats of
Atkyns' 'neighbours and countrymen' included in the book, show not
only the architectural details of the houses, but also the layout of the
gardens and the arrangement of the paths that made such a significant
contribution to the formality and symmetry of these gardens. All the
paths were straight, and the principal ones were about 8ft wide, with a
surface of sand or gravel and grass borders of equal width. The sand and
gravel surfaces gave a colour contrast to the plantings, and enabled the
path to be used in wet weather without causing damage by trampling.

Westbury Court Gardens. A reconstructed parterre. The original parterres at Westbury
were overlooked from the pavilion.

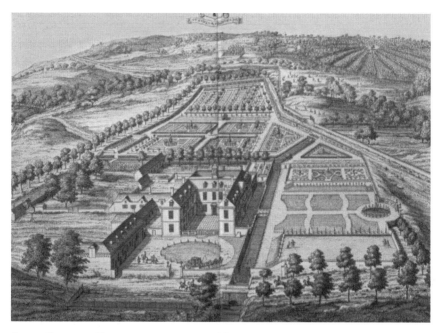

Cassey Compton. The Kip engraving was published in 1712. The raised walkways are to the right of the house.

The gravel surface also reflected sun light, and this was important for the ripening of fruit on the nearby trees. Sixty houses are illustrated in Atkyns' book and a common feature of many of their gardens is the elaborate and intricate parterre. 'Improbably complex' Timothy Mowl describes them. Although the engravings are stylised and drawn to enhance the status of the house owners, the labour and expenditure in maintaining these exuberant parterres was undoubtedly great. They almost demanded viewpoints from which they could be overlooked and their designs more fully appreciated. Coloured earth, powdered clay tiles, charcoal and yellow sand were used to fill in the box-edged patterns of some parterres, and in other examples a variety of flowers or clipped evergreens were planted on hump backed or 'carp back' beds within the box frameworks. Plantings were not allowed to be so tall as to obscure the view of the patterns. An impression of what they looked like may be obtained from the National Trust's reconstructed parterre at Westbury Court. The oblique aerial views of Kip's engravings enable the patterns to be clearly seen, but for viewing from ground level a terrace helps. So where the house

was at a distance from the parterres, or where tall pavilions were not provided, the parterres and bowling greens were often bordered by narrow
terraces from which the garden design could be more readily admired.
It is not easy to pick out these raised walkways in the engravings, we
have to look for the carefully drawn steps to find them. A good example,
for which there is still evidence today, may be seen at Cassey Compton,
that remote country house between Withington and the Chedworth
Roman villa. Here, beside the south front lawn, are earthen banks supporting rows of large shaggy yew trees. In the early eighteenth-century
engraving, one bank is shown as a raised walkway with small clipped
evergreens, alternately conical and round, and presumably the same yews
that we see today. From this raised path the beautiful embroidery pattern could be viewed. The other bank overlooks the bowling green, now
the site of a Dutch barn. Once we have identified this type of terrace
walk in one of Kip's engravings, we can more quickly recognise others.
At Kempsford by the Thames is Lady Maud's Walk, and at Dyrham the
grassed slope north east of the house was also once terraced in this way,
and there are nine others in the Atkyns' collection. Sometimes Kip draws
couples strolling in the gardens, occasionally a single gentleman with his
walking stick, but more often the symbolic carriage and six or individual
horse riders are seen arriving at the house.

Another common feature of the engravings, which soon began to
dominate the layout of country estates, is the avenue of trees leading to
a distant summer house, an ornamental wrought-iron gate, or simply to
the edge of the estate. The Kip engraving of Westbury Court shows an
avenue of oak trees extending to the south east of the garden. Counting
the number of trees in the drawing and comparing this with the number
bought by Maynard Colchester, as recorded in his account book for making the garden, we find a discrepancy of one. Perhaps Kip also consulted
the account book! These avenues not only gave the opportunity for rid-
ing or walking to the estate boundaries, but they were also conspicuous
visible signs of great landownership. And where a lesser neighbouring
landowner could be persuaded to plant his avenues or clumps of trees
along the same alignment, the impression was even greater! Many country houses still possess avenues of lime, beech and horse chestnut trees,
and at one time elm was another popular tree for this type of planting.

For the most extensive development of avenues we go to Cirencester
Park. Here, in the early eighteenth century, Allen Bathurst together

The Broad Walk, Cirencester Park. It stretches for six miles to Sapperton.

The Rococo Garden, Painswick House.

with his friend Alexander Pope 'combined to produce the largest area of early Georgian landscape layout to survive in Britain'. Of particular fame is the Broad Walk which eventually stretched for six miles between Cirencester and Sapperton. It is about 50yds wide, across gently undulating country and partly bordered by planted oak, beech, and chestnut trees, and partly cut through the older Oakley Wood. There is also a sprinkling of other trees such as cherry, yew and a variety of conifers to provide seasonal colouring. Its survival is due both to the forestry expertise of Lord Bathurst, which ensured the establishment of a commercially profitable woodland estate, and to his longevity, which prevented it from succumbing to succeeding landscaping fashions. The earl managed his inherited estate for seventy-one years and Oakley Wood, which he purchased, for fifty-nine years. The Broad Walk was aligned to Cirencester church, rather than to the main house, and some of the rides which lead from it were also aligned to nearby churches. Its scale is massive and rather dwarfs the trees and the ornamental buildings that are dotted along the sides of its course. Along the Broad Walk and the other avenues Lord Bathurst used to ride for two hours a day, and many generations of horse riders and walkers have enjoyed the privilege of access to the grounds in the years since his time. Later plans of the estate show a small band along the border of the Park, north-west of the house, where the narrow paths through the trees are more serpentine. Here was a Rococo garden.

For a brief period around the 1740s, Rococo gardens were in fashion. There had been a reaction against the stiffness and rigidity of the formal gardens, and before long the landscaping designs of William Kent, Launcelot Brown, Humphrey Repton and their followers swept away most evidence of their former existence. Fortunately, the appearance of the eighteenth-century Rococo gardens has been preserved by the paintings of Thomas Robins. An area of Gloucester between Longsmith Street and Commercial Road was once the garden of Marybone House, home of Benjamin Hyett. Robins painted it with its winding paths, pagoda and numerous visitors. Then, a few years later, Hyett created another similar garden at what is now Painswick House. The site of this garden in a steep sided valley was not conducive to later garden designs and the bones of the rococo layout survived beneath the trees and shrubs that eventually grew over it until work on its restoration began in the early 1980s, using Robins' 1748 painting as a guide. Through a doorway in the brick wall behind the house, the visitor is presented with a view over most of the garden, but the paths lead left and right to a variety of built structures such as the Gothick Red House, the pink Eagle House and the white Exedra, and with many playful surprises along the way. Some paths are straight, others winding, and although there is some symmetry in the diamond-shaped and productive fruit and vegetable garden in the centre, there is much less than characterised the earlier designs. It is a colourful, disjointed, complex garden, with many diversions. Thomas Robins' paintings do not have the amazingly accurate perspective of Kip's engravings, but they have in compensation elaborate wide borders decorated with shells and flowers, birds and butterflies. The term 'rococo' from the French *rocaille* and the Portuguese *barroco*, used for the gardens he illustrated, admirably suits his style. It has been suggested that he may have had some influence on Hyett's garden layouts.

Neither William Kent nor Lancelot Brown had much direct control of Gloucestershire gardens. Kent worked on park buildings at Badminton, and has two beautifully carved gate piers with swags where the old lime avenue reaches the present A40 at Great Barrington. Brown was responsible for the lay out of Dodington Park. Humphrey Repton had

Repton's layout of the Thornery, Sezincote House.

more influence, though often in an advisory capacity. He was dubbed 'the walk maker' by his critics and in his famous Red Books, which described and illustrated an estate before and after he had worked on it, there was normally a section headed 'walks'. In the typical Repton land-scape garden there were two drives, one short and functional, leading directly from the road to the house, the other designed to show off the estate. The latter was planned to give a succession of views, allowing the eye to choose what to look at rather than being forced to see an obelisk or temple at the end of an avenue. He wrote that he took great care in planning the 'direction of every road or walk, that we may compel the most careless to observe those parts of a design, which have a claim upon their admiration'. Cuttings, banks and shrub plantings bordered the drive, and at intervals clearings and gaps gave the opportunity for the desired views. The drive was winding to lead the eye onwards and much longer than the service road, and in the case of Blaize Castle near Bristol, 1 ½ miles compared to 100yds! From the drives, which were primarily for carriages but could also be followed on foot, gravel walks led to the garden's attractive features – perhaps to a cave, a view point, a seat, or a bridge over a tumbling stream. Glades of fine mown turf were designed

A lily-covered lake at Adlestrop.

for invalid chairs, where a gravel walk would have been too noisy and bumpy, and Repton even considered what surface was most appropriate for a lady's satin shoes. Sound was another important component of the garden experience and this was usually provided by the running water of a carefully controlled stream, where water was allowed to cascade over imported rock outcrops. Colourful flowers were also emphasised, and plant hunters had by now introduced many exotic species. The paths were designed to give access to them for detailed botanical examination. The water garden at Sezincote, known as the Thornery, has a winding gravel path with stepping stones that invites such an inspection. The path repeatedly crosses the narrow stream, which has been channelled between moss and fern covered rocks, by a succession of small stone bridges. The skyline is dominated by several 200-year-old cedars of Lebanon and some unusually contorted oaks. The planting of introduced shrubs, bulbs and herbaceous plants brings colour and variety at all seasons, and the garden is set within a parkland of fine trees and near an elongated lake designed to look like a broad river. Although there is also a more recent formal garden of Moghul symbolism, much at Sezincote retains the marks of Repton's hand. Timothy Mowl, the garden historian, has helpfully compared this garden with the similar one of shallow artificial waterfalls, winding paths, and fine cedars set in parkland, that was once the shared view of both Adlestrop House and Adlestrop Park, homes of members of the Leigh family. Here, too, a small stream has been dammed to give two long lakes, the lower one strikingly lit in summer by white water lilies.

Large churchyards became popular places in which to walk in the early nineteenth century. A common pastime on a summer evening was for small groups of ladies to stroll along the network of paths amongst the tombs and yew trees, to read the epitaphs of their predecessors inscribed upon the grave stones, and to reflect on their lives of long ago, of their achievements and tragedies, of their hopes and promises. A particularly appropriate context for this was the churchyard at Painswick, with its notable collection of elegantly carved clothiers' table tombs and clipped yew trees. The latter, originally planted in 1792, now include far more than the legendary ninety-nine, possibly as many as 138. And many similar country church paths still invite the walker.

At the end of the nineteenth and into the early twentieth centuries a new type of garden layout became fashionable. In this, the house was

Mrs Winthrop's garden, Hidcote.

The troughery at Rodmarton Manor.

seemingly extended into the garden by a series of garden rooms, each with its distinctive character, and separated from the others by walls or hedges. One garden might be developed around a lily pool or a specimen tree, another centred on a rockery, another with herbaceous borders. Inviting glimpses of the adjoining garden rooms could be seen through gateways or gaps in the hedges, but the linkage was by paths of brick, stone paving or mown grass. The variety of soil and micro-climatic conditions, created in these small enclosed areas, enabled a much wider range of flowers to be grown than was previously possible. They were gardens in which individual plants were given greater prominence. The best-known example is probably the National Trust garden at Hidcote in the north of the county, but the gardens at Snowshill Manor and Rodmarton Manor also well illustrate the style of the Arts and Crafts movement. At Hidcote, where work on the garden began 100 years ago when the property was bought by Mrs Gertrude Winthrop and was developed by her son Major Lawrence Johnston, there are fifteen garden rooms off the two main axes without any obviously planned sequence. Many rare plants were introduced from the plant hunting expeditions

Major Johnston undertook or supported. Some of these have now gone, and the vivid colours of beds of flowers, set off by yew and box, hornbeam and holly hedges, dominate the scene. The connecting paths here can scarcely take the crowds of visitors on a summer weekend. The grass walks need protection in wet weather, but the paths of brick, gravel, stone sets and flagstones are better able to withstand the wear and tear. Recent restoration work has included reinstating the cobbled paths of the East Court, and has entailed a search for bricks of the right colour, size and age for Mrs Winthrop's Garden. At Rodmarton Manor the garden was designed so that the garden rooms became less formal with increasing distance from the house. In one of them, the seventeenth-century idea of a raised path overlooking the parterres has been inverted, the garden plants have been raised above the level of the paths by being planted in stone troughs. Delicate alpines and other small plants may be appreciated more easily this way.

The municipal gardens of our towns also incorporate paths in their layout. Here the design usually reflects the space available, the landscaping fashions at the date at which the garden was formed and, in latter years, the cost of maintenance. The siting of seats, litter bins and access points determines the degree of wear and tear of the grass, and quickly reveals the effectiveness or otherwise of the path layout.

More recently, with the growing interest in nature conservation, wild gardens have become popular. Here, paths are of grass or chipped bark, and wind between trees and shrubs. Native wild flowers are grown and habitats for birds and insects are created. The path is designed to give quiet access, with minimum disturbance to the natural scene. Another disturbing modern trend has been the expansion of gravel, paved, tarmac and concrete paths to cover the whole front gardens of many estate houses. This enables cars and other vehicles to be parked off the road but has negative environmental consequences. Because these materials readily absorb solar radiation, surface temperatures are increased, the opportunities for plant and wildlife are diminished and rain water runs off the surface rather than infiltrating the soil, thus contributing to increased flood risk after intense rainfall.

So garden paths have a range of purposes. They have been used to give structure to the garden, by dividing it into distinct plots, and they gave access routes for the gardeners and their wheelbarrows. Their design has influenced the speed of movement of visitors, from a brisk walk for physical exercise, to a gentle stroll to appreciate the colours, forms and scents of the plants. Different surfaces not only gave colour variety but also provided contrasting walking conditions, ranging from soft springy turf, through loose gravel, to hard stone. Sunshine and shade was controlled by the spacing of trees bordering the path, and a sense of formality or naturalness was conveyed by the straightness or the curves of the path. Some paths encouraged an outward emphasis by leading to view points overlooking distant scenes, others were more introspective, encouraging meditation and reflection, and focussing on the more intimate aspects of life. The path has one of the most important roles in garden design and the great gardens of Gloucestershire clearly demonstrate this significance.

For further reading: Timothy Mowl *Historic Gardens of Gloucestershire* Tempus 2002.

NINE

A Walking Tour of the Forest of Dean – 100 Years Ago

In this chapter and the next we will look at some longer paths that have been followed in leisure walking, first in the Forest of Dean and then along the Cotswold edge. We begin by analysing an early walker's guide, noticing the recommended routes and what was to be seen in those days and commenting on the subsequent changes in the landscape.

Just before the First World War, the London publisher, Constable, produced the first detailed guide to the Forest of Dean★. In the opinion of the author, A.O. Cooke, walking was the best means of travel to reveal the beauty and antiquarian interests of this little-known region. Motorists moved too quickly, they arrived 'cloaked, goggled and veiled', stopped for a few minutes, and then rattled off creating clouds of dust. Cyclists were generally restricted to made-up roads, and so missed much of interest. 'The one true way of seeing Dean Forest is to go afoot'. And a major advantage for a walking tour in those days was that there was a railway network with numerous small stations. Although the trains were slow and infrequent, 'keeping pace with a butterfly' F.W. Harvey has suggested, and the winding tracks were liable to unseat the unwary passenger too intent on enjoying the views from the carriage window, trains made it possible for walks to be linear rather than circular, and they were frequently used by Cooke either for the outward or the return journey.

Two hotels were convenient bases for these walks. The Speech House at the traditional heart of the Forest (the obelisk marking its centre is by the roadside opposite) was the most suitable, but the Victoria Hotel at Newnham could also be used for exploring the eastern margins of the Forest and Severnside. So the stations at Speech House Road and

Newnham were usually those through which Cooke passed for the day's walk.

Twenty walks are described, mostly taken in spring and summer, but as he lived near Chepstow, the author knew the area at all seasons and appreciated its beauty in autumn and winter as well. Clear instructions are given for the recommended routes, with alternative suggestions when time and energy were limiting factors. Most can be followed with ease today, although the well made Forestry Commission roads often seem more inviting than those that Cooke recommends. The forestry roads were substantially improved by allied forces during the Second World War, when heavy military vehicles and munitions were stored in the Forest, but in Cooke's time the horse-drawn wagons, used in hauling timber out of the Forest, had left ruts sometimes as deep as 3ft. All the paths radiating from the Speech House were followed, and journeys were made to Highmeadow Woods, Symonds Yat, New Beechenhurst, Ruardean, Newnham, Lydney, Blackpool Brook and Parkend. From Newnham walks were to Westbury, Flaxley, Littledean, Bream, Lydney and Beachley. Finally a walk was followed from Chepstow through St Briavels, Clearwell and Newland, to Staunton and the Wye valley. On two occasions he arranged to walk with woodmen and their company was recommended as a valuable source of information because of their more intimate knowledge of the Forest. Two walks are mentioned as 'not to be missed', one follows the ridge at Edge Hills east of Cinderford, the other goes down the slope from Blaize Bailey to Newnham. But many other walks are described as delightful. The ridge walk at Edge Hills is now a hard Forestry Commission road and not so pleasant to walk along, but just below the ridge, paths lead to the shafts of old iron mines from which mules carried iron ore down to Cinderford in the nineteenth century. In spring time, with the bluebells in flower, the fresh green foliage of the birch trees and the call of the cuckoo, it is difficult to imagine the heavy industrial scene here in the decades leading up to Cooke's walk.

He recommended that thick boots be worn because of the dewy grass and boggy tracks, and that old and sombre-coloured clothes were more appropriate than summer frocks and elegant light flannel suits. The reason for the latter advice was that coal miners used the same footpaths on their journeys home from the pits and left coal dust and mud on the red-painted stiles and gates as they did so. Flies were also a problem in July and August, and tobacco smoke was a useful deterrent – though a

The Three Brothers, Russell's Bank. Only one is still alive.

possible fire hazard! Warnings were given about the dangers of exploring alone the ancient iron mines or scowles, with their hidden crevices; of the need for a guide if the caves along the sides of the Wye valley were to be entered; of the treacherous tides of the lower Severn when fossil hunting along its cliff shores, and of the ease of getting lost in Highmeadow Woods.

In describing the routes, Cooke draws attention to those features that he thought a tourist would find interesting, and these often determined the paths taken. Ancient trees, spectacular views, old houses, churches and crosses were chief among them, but he was also aware of the need to avoid over-prescription and wanted to encourage visitors to make their own personal discoveries of other 'charms'.

Precise directions are given to enable the visitor to find the oldest oak trees in the Forest. Jack o' the Yat was beside the Gloucester – Monmouth road, close to the entrance to Sallow Vallets Lodge, and the Crad Oak could be found beside a track 300yds south of this lodge. Its dead trunk stands there today. The Three Brothers were at a junction of tracks north of Russell's Bank, with only one alive today, and the oldest and largest of all, the Newland Oak with a girth of 44ft, was even then a hollow ruin in a field north of the parish church. Most mature oaks in the Forest were then less than 100 years old, and Cooke distinguished between the sessile oak, which gave straight timber, and the more branching pedunculate oak, which was planted for ship timber. Many of the older oaks had stags heads, which he thought was because insufficient water was available to the trees. There were also a few very large beech trees to be seen in Beech Avenue, north east of Coleford. Many forest inclosures had an understorey of beech, which was then thought to be beneficial to the growth of the oaks. Near the Speech House and beside the remains of Highmeadow House, the air in May was fragrant from the blossom of hawthorns. Other deciduous trees, which made a significant contribution to the beauty of the Forest, were sweet chestnuts in the Vale of Castiard at Flaxley, elms by the Wye at the Biblins, lime avenues at Dean Hall and Naas House, and birch, which rapidly colonised the waste tips of the coal mines and provided useful planks for the floors of the stone-carrying carts. Scattered cherry trees with their snowy, foam-like blossom brightened the gloom of the evergreen plantings.

Spruce was the most valued conifer at the time, and the trees in the Spruce Drive south of the Speech House, which were planted in 1837, were then 60ft high, creating a long, sombre and largely silent, aromatic path towards Staple-edge, a path which Cooke walked on several tours. These spruces have all been felled. The other commercially important conifer was the larch, which, despite its insect pests, grew rapidly for a good cash return, and provided a cool damp environment for the young oak trees in mixed plantings. Ancient yew trees graced the churchyards at Abenhall and Awre, and their roots clasped the jagged blocks of rock in the scowles and on the limestone cliffs along the Wye – they still do. Gnarled old holly trees were numerous around the Speech House and they too are common here at the present day.

At the time when the book was written, the woods were managed locally for the Crown. The Forestry Commission was not established until 1919, and only took responsibility for work in the Forest of Dean in 1924. So the widespread block planting of a greater variety of conifers, which was the Commission's early policy, had not yet taken place. The new species, which often came from western North America, soon began to dominate the Forest until amenity values became more appreciated and the Commission realised that these conifers could be grown in many other parts of Britain. Land in the possession of the

View over the Severn Valley from Pleasant Stile above Newnham.

Forestry Commission that was suitable for broadleaf trees was much more restricted, and the Dean was one such area and is now planted accordingly.

The hilly terrain of the Forest provided many notable viewpoints. The Duke of Wellington is even reputed to have declined the offer of the Highmeadow estate because the view west reminded him too much of the Pyrenees! Cooke's walks included visits to the flag poles sited at the highest view points at Ruardean Hill and the Buckstone, to the eastern edge of the Forest overlooking the Severn Valley from the Wilderness and Pleasant Stile, to the western edge overlooking the Wye valley from Symonds Yat, the most famous and most frequented view point, and the Devil's Pulpit high above Tintern. Ruardean village and Near Harkening Rock were other destinations chosen for their panoramas. Lower viewpoints included Pope's Hill, the old Severn railway viaduct at Purton, and the cliff tops at Westbury, Newnham and Sedbury. He noted how the Forest lodges, in addition to their attractive gardens and tree nurseries, also had pleasant views, although tree growth sometimes eventually restricted these. He climbed the tower of Tidenham church and on to the roof of St Briavels Castle for the views there, and considered the coal waste tips useful in this respect. That of the New Fancy colliery may still

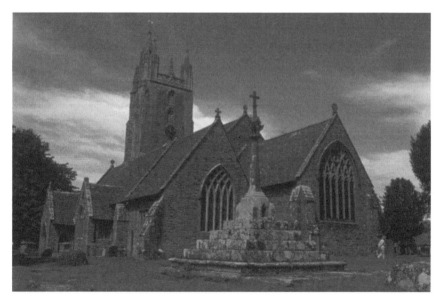

Newland church and cross. The church contains the famous miner's brass.

The fourteenth-century cross at Clearwell.

be appreciated in this way.

The Crown forest was managed from lodges. There were originally six lodges dating from the seventeenth century, and they were later increased to include one for each main inclosure. Here, walkers could obtain refreshments, including tea and cider, and had opportunities to talk to the woodmen. The Speech House, built between 1668 and 1680 and then extended in 1883, was one of the first. It was possible in Cooke's time to arrive unannounced, to be welcomed and then shown round old privately owned houses and he reports visits to Flaxley Abbey, Stuare Farm (then known as Steers), Dean Hall, Poulton Court, Drake's House at Gatcombe, Purton Manor, Naas House and St Briavels Castle. He also viewed the exterior and gardens of Westbury Court, Lydney Park and Clanna. Some houses were sketched for the book by J. W. King, and where there were special scenic opportunities for the photographer or artist, they were noted.

The churches within the Forest boundary such as Christ Church at Berry Hill only date from the early nineteenth century, but around the Forest periphery are many ancient ones. Two in particular were found to be of great antiquarian interest – Newland with its miner's brass and tomb of John Wyrrall, a fifteenth-century Forester-of-Fee, and Staunton with

Wire putchers and old boats by the former quay at Gatcombe.

its very early Norman font. But the attractions of many other churches were also noted, such as the stone-carved devices of the free smiths and free miners at Abenhall, the sculptured St George and the Dragon on the tympanum above the doorway at Ruardean, the massive oak timbers in the detached shingled spire at Westbury, and the fifteenth-century doom painting on oak panels above the chancel screen at Mitcheldean. Churches and old houses were conceived to be major tourist attractions at the time. Cooke agreed with the opinion that Steers, near Newnham, was the finest house of the Forest, and he thought Staunton church was the most interesting building in the whole tour. He also noted the four-teenth-century stone crosses at Lydney, Aylburton, Clearwell, Newland and Staunton, commenting on the shapes and numbers of steps of their bases and on their niches.

Various workmen were encountered on the walks. Their methods of working were carefully observed, and in some cases tried out. He helped fell an oak tree with axe and saw, watched and copied the bark strip-pers at work prising away the oak bark for subsequent use in leather tanning, shared refreshments with charcoal burners and learned about salmon fishing in the Severn whether by putchers, the wine-bottle shaped wicker baskets held on racks in the river, or by the triangular 'stop' nets lowered from anchored boats. At Gatcombe a few old fishing boats and some wire putchers may be seen beside the former quay and at Newnham details of these traditional methods of fishing are displayed in the fishermen's hut by the Severn.

In the woods near Bream, and also near Clearwell and in Abbot's Wood near Littledean he visited the scowles, entering the gloom of their trenches. These are sometimes as much as 70ft deep, with yew and beech trees overhanging their limestone sides.

He often followed the old tramways, by which stone, iron ore and coal had been transported in the past, and frequently crossed the min-eral railway lines, which were then in use as their successors. Among the recently constructed features of the landscape that he mentions were the Crown roads, which were not yet included on the Ordnance Survey maps, and which today form part of the scenic motorist routes by Cannop ponds and towards Symonds Yat. However, of greater interest to Cooke were the so-called Roman roads. He doubted the validity of all the examples of 'traces of Roman pavement' shown on the old OS maps, but one whole day's walk was devoted to following the ancient

The ancient road at Blackpool Bridge. Notice the signs of a diversion towards the bridge.

road which is exposed for about 50yds, with its curb stones, sets and fragments of a diversion, at Blackpool Bridge. It was then possible to trace it from Sutton Bottom through to the Yorkley-Lydney road, with paving stones at the surface in several places. The details of its origin are now less certain and the simple designation 'Ancient Road' is probably more accurate.

Yet the beauty of the Forest was not undiluted. Coal mining was conspicuous, with numerous waste tips and pit head gear at the collieries – at least ten working mines were passed. There was a visible legacy of the recently important iron industry in cinder heaps and derelict buildings, which had not yet been cleared. Streams were polluted – black with water pumped from coal mines in the case of Blackpool Brook, ruddy with waste from the tin-plate works, and dead as a result of effluent from the papermills. Over Lydney, Lydbrook and Redbrook hung persistent dark clouds of smoke from the tin-plate works. Housing in the drab and bare mining villages was often ugly and of poor quality, and even in the more attractive villages away from the mining areas, such as Newland, some houses had been given roofs of clay tiles or slates, rather than the traditional stone, and a garish red wash of the walls was becoming popular. He thought Cinderford expressed the Forest at its visual worst and that the size of the workhouse at Westbury was inappropriate for a small village – though later it had a very significant role in the miners' strike of 1926, when it provided daily meals for the destitute women and children who were prepared to walk four or five miles for them. The broken road surface and inches of white dust caused by traction engines pulling cement trucks from Mitcheldean to Lea station were also unpleasant features in that area. However, not all the features introduced by industry were blots on the landscape. Ponds and lakes, originally designed to provide water power, contributed to the interest of the area. They enabled trout fishing and the observation of wildlife, and when drained, as at Flaxley, gave lush meadows. The delights of the Forest far outweighed the blemishes.

There were no deer in the Forest at the time. These had been deliberately eliminated in the 1850s – which raises a question about the age of the antlers displayed in the Court Room at the Speech House, and illustrated in the book. There were few rabbits, hares were common, and

A spectacular display of bluebells in the Iron Age fort on Welshbury Hill.

The tallest foxgloves grow on Staunton Meend.

birds of prey such as owls and hawks were protected because of their control of the rodents that would normally damage young trees. Pigs fed on acorns and beech mast in the autumn, and sheep, made grey by coal dust, wore bells round their necks. The tinkling music indicated their whereabouts to the commoners. The seasonal display of flowers, with bluebells in May especially at Welshbury and the Russells Inclosure, foxgloves in July when the tallest grew on the sandy lower slopes of Staunton Meend, ferns on the limestone outcrops and gorse on the sandstone, and the rust colour of bracken in the autumn, delighted him. These may still be enjoyed, and although the planting of conifers on parts of Welshbury Hill has curtailed the bluebell display, beneath the limes and beeches around the Iron Age fort on the crown of the hill it remains spectacular in late April and early May. Highmeadow Woods, where the mature oak trees were at their finest and few visitors came, was the prime location for flowers and butterflies. Here lily-of-the-valley was abundant, wild columbine and rare orchids were found, and the purple emperor and wood white butterflies could be seen. In fact thirty-six different species of butterfly had been recorded here.

Cooke enjoyed the apparent social amity of Newnham, where large houses, humble cottages and shops were intermingled along the colour-

St Anthony's Well, near Greenbottom.

ful High Street, the blossom of Blakeney Red pears – a local variety for making perry, the beech-shaded St Anthony's Well near Greenbottom, and the slab of quartz conglomerate of the Buckstone. He tells us that the latter had been a logan stone which could be rocked by four men in 1804, by two to three in 1852, and by one in 1881. It was eventually dislodged in 1885 by some touring actors, and subsequently returned to near its original position and anchored there by the Crown authorities. The locations of gruesome events associated with the Civil War were recorded as the tour proceeded, as were prehistoric or Roman camps and monastic granges.

Campers were met at the Biblins in the Wye valley, and boat trippers from Ross to Monmouth were spotted along the Wye, but mention was made of no other walking tourists. These were early days for general walking in the Forest, and the outbreak of the First World War would soon further curtail such leisurely pursuits. Paths were not waymarked then, nor were there the provisions made for other tourists such as the cycle tracks, car parks, picnic places, toilets and advertised commercial attractions that we find today. And although a Sunday afternoon walk was popular at the time, only the more affluent and leisured classes could spare whole days for such pursuits. It was towards such a readership that the book was addressed. It was too large and heavy for a pocket guide, so its detailed route descriptions would have had to be memorised, or copied on paper. And some descriptions could only be appreciated by an armchair reader who was already very familiar with the Forest. But it gives an informed insight into leisure walking 100 years ago and provides a basis for comparison with today's ramblers' routes and attractions.

The most popular walks in the Forest now are those circular routes marked by posts with coloured arrows which have been designed by the Forestry Commission and centred on the main car parks. These clearly defined trails may be confidently followed and take the visitor to a variety of landscape features. But they also serve another important purpose. Because these paths absorb most visitors who want to walk in the Forest, the conservation of the rest of the woodland is made easier. And since people generally walk no further than about 100 yards from their cars, environmental damage, wear and tear, and litter are largely confined to this radius. Again, the numbers of visitors to these popular sites can be managed and restricted to their 'carrying capacities' by controlling the size of the car parks. Symonds Yat, Beechenhurst, Speech House, Mallards Pike and Wenchford take most of this pressure, and here the typical tourist amenities are provided. The Dean Heritage Centre at Soudley is another honeypot for visitors.

The old railway lines that Cooke once travelled are now used by cyclists, who have much wider access to the Forest than they did in his day. There are, however, the longer walks waymarked by the Ramblers Association and the two county wide trails, the Gloucestershire Way and the Wysis Way, that give experiences closer to those that Cooke so greatly enjoyed 100 years ago.

★ A small earlier volume had been published by John Bellows entitled *A Week's Holiday in the Forest of Dean.*

TEN

The Thirteenth National Trail – Walking the Cotswold Way

It may seem strange to include a chapter on the Cotswold Way in a book on old paths. But after a few moments reflection, we realise that this too is an old path and links together footpaths and bridleways that existed long before May 1970, when the long distance path was first designated. In fact, it could be claimed to be the oldest we have considered, because parts date back to the Iron Age, if not before, and other sections follow a medieval wool-pack route.

When H.J. Massingham wrote *Cotswold Country* in 1937, he made a perceptive distinction between the Wolds and the Edge. The Wolds were characterised as rolling country, with stone-walled fields accommodating flocks of sheep or crops of wheat and barley, grey stone villages clustered around church and manor house, and gently flowing trout streams. Scattered small woods were fox coverts and the parks of the country houses were made ornamental by clumps of beech trees and avenues of limes. The Edge was different. It had much steeper gradients, not only on the scarp face itself but also on the sides of the combes and bottoms that have been cut into it. Cattle were more common here, with both beef and dairy herds, and there were extensive strips of beech woodland on the upper slopes. There is little cultivation today, although traces of ridge and furrow show that this was not always the case. At intervals along the escarpment are broad stretches of common land, sometimes acquired for golf courses, and often with the prehistoric remains of long barrows, tumuli and hill forts. And here on the steeper slopes the traditional limestone flowers still flourish. Farming is less prosperous along the Edge and the opportunities for intensive farming are much more restricted than further east, so many farmers have accepted grants under the various stewardship schemes for environmentally friendly farming. The Wolds are associated with skylarks and hares, while the Edge has buzzards and badgers. Today, there is a clearer distinction between Edge and Wold than there was in Massingham's time.

The Cotswold Way is an Edge path. It generally follows the top of the escarpment, descending from time to time into the vale to pass through spring-line villages and market towns, but then climbing back to the top again for yet another extensive view over the Severn valley to the Malverns, the Forest of Dean, and far beyond. It has recently been upgraded to the status of a National Trail extending from Chipping Campden in the north to Bath in the south. As in the previous chapter, we will not describe the route because there are several books that do this most adequately, but we will focus on the features that have made this path such a popular one for leisure walking, considering both natural and man made elements of the landscape, and we begin with some comments on its geology and landforms.

From the many disused quarries along the top of the escarpment we can gain an insight into the geological characteristics of the Inferior Oolite, which outcrops here. The Leckhampton quarries have probably

An exposure of the Freestone beds of the Inferior Oolite, Leckhampton Quarry.

been the most significant for building materials, for from them came the stone used in the development of Regency Cheltenham. Most of the building stones were cut to shape in the quarries when fresh, and then transported downhill by plateway. The inclines of several of these former plateways may still be seen. Lime for mortar was also obtained from the quarries. But the Leckhampton quarries were not only important in Cheltenham's history, they have great significance for geologists because exposed in the quarry faces is an almost complete sequence of rocks of the Inferior Oolite and conservation work has made all the beds accessible for closer inspection. The uniform beds with widely spaced bedding planes and joints are those of the Upper and Lower Freestone. These provided the main building stones which were easily cut into ashlar blocks for Cheltenham houses. Sometimes the Freestone shows current bedding, where waves in the shallow seas in which the rock was formed caused ripples in the sediment as it accumulated. Between these two beds is the Oolite Marl, a mixture of hard and soft rock containing many brachiopod fossils. Beneath the Lower Freestone is Pea Grit. This is also fossiliferous, but mainly distinguished by its pea-sized nodules set in a cement and shell debris matrix. We meet it again on Crickley Hill. Above the Upper Freestone and covering the top of the Hill are layers of the Trigonia Grits, Notgrove Freestone and Griphyte Grit. The grits are not true grits, but shelly limestones, and produce rough, rubbly stones sometimes used to decorate buildings because of their large, white fossils. A wide shallow quarry east of the Iron Age camp on Leckhampton Hill known as Brownstones Quarry once provided stone for garden rockeries, walls and minor road surfaces. This site has now been reclaimed for agricultural use but the quarry edges may be followed around the field. The nobbly surface of the paths on the highest levels is partly caused by Gryphaea fossils. Gryphaea bilobata is a type of oyster. The three quarries where the Inferior Oolite sequence may be examined are Lime Kilns, Deadman's and Brownstone, and for those with an interest in geology the slight deviation from the Cotswold Way is worthwhile. Good fossil specimens may be picked up from the loose scree and spoil without the need to hammer at the quarry face. The Devil's Chimney just below Deadman's Quarry is a column of Lower Freestone left by the quarrymen and now conserved as an important Cheltenham landmark. The Cotswold Way also passes above Salterley Grange Quarry, where again the structural features of the Lower Freestone may be clearly seen. Easily accessible exposures of Inferior Oolite may be inspected on Cleeve Hill, Painswick Beacon, Scottsquar Hill near Edge and Coaley Peak, and there are working quarries at Fish Hill above Broadway and near Stumps Cross, but those at Leckhampton are the most instructive for the geologist.

Another rock making a significant contribution to the landscape of the Cotswold edge is to be seen near Stinchcombe. Some of the buildings here and at North Nibley are of Marlstone, a hard, fine-grained, silty limestone. The grains are coated with limonite, which gives the stone its buff rusty colour, the colour of gingerbread, and its mica flakes glint in the sunlight. The rock's resistance to erosion has produced a platform at about the 120m contour along the scarp face from Stinchcombe to Wotton-under-Edge, which can be seen to best advantage at North Nibley when viewed from Stinchcombe Hill. Stone has been quarried on the north-west side of this hill and the soil derived from it is very fertile. Near Wotton-under-Edge market gardens have been developed on it. Smaller ledges of Marlstone may also be seen on Robinswood Hill, near Gloucester.

Most of the scarp face consists of sands and clays, and can be very wet in winter, especially where springs issue along the slope. In some places

View of the Marlstone ledge at North Nibley from Stinchcombe Hill, with the Tyndale monument on the hill above.

such as below Barrow Wake and south of Broadway the corrugations of ridge and furrow show where cultivation in medieval times climbed to much higher levels than today, even to near the top of the escarpment. And near Farmcote and Wotton-under-Edge the terraces of strip lynchets are conspicuous. Here, ploughing along the contours has loosened the soil to allow it to move down hill under gravity. At the lower side of the ploughed strip it accumulated, giving the terrace form. In places the upper slopes are covered with low hummocks. Within each hummock is a much weathered block of Oolitic limestone, which was split off from the outcrop at the top of the escarpment and slid down the slope over the frozen subsurface in periglacial conditions. Shallow soil now covers these blocks, and because of its warm, well drained, calcareous quality it supports small islands of typical Cotswold flowers such as cowslips, rock rose and harebells.

The steep-sided bays that have been scalloped out of the scarp face are known as combes. They sometimes correspond to fault lines where the rock has been weakened and the gravel, which has been washed out of the combes, is often spread over the lowland in front of them. Witcombe and Harescombe are good examples. In the south, beyond Dursley, valleys penetrate far into the escarpment. These are the 'bottoms' with their characteristic land use pattern of pasture beside the streams, woods on the upper slopes, and arable farming on the plateau above.

Where the streams issuing from the Cotswolds are widely spaced, and where the rocks have been more resistant to erosion, conspicuous outliers occur. Churchdown Hill and Robinswood Hill are mainly shaped by Marlstone but Cam Long Down, which the Cotswold Way climbs, has not been completely separated from the escarpment rocks and is capped by Oolitic limestone. This produces its flat top, in contrast to the adjacent Peaked Down where the beautifully symmetrical cone shape results from the uniform erosion of the exposed sands and clays.

The Cotswold edge has many notable prehistoric remains. On the promontories are a series of Iron Age hill forts, in fact the Cotswold Way, for much of its route, follows the prehistoric track that once linked these forts. The hill forts seem to fall into two groups. These are distinguished by their size, the construction of their ramparts, and the pottery discovered within them. Those of the early Iron Age are dated between 700 BC and 400 BC and are smaller, with ramparts constructed of dry-stone walling held together with timber lacing, and have pottery decorated by incised

The Iron Age fort on Crickley Hill, from Barrow Wake.

lines and finger nail patterns. They were genuine defensive camps, protected naturally or by fortifications all round, and excavations have shown them to have been attacked and burnt down. Of these Crickley is the most researched site and here there have been many seasons of archaeological excavations. Information boards give some insight into the appearance of the settlements and coloured markers indicate the position of the post holes of the houses and show that an earlier group of rectangular huts was followed by the circular huts of a later occupation of the site. The hill forts that the Cotswold Way passes at Shenberrow above Stanton, Beckbury above Hailes, Cleeve Cloud and Leckhampton also belong to this early series.

The second group dates from around 400 BC. These hill forts are visually more impressive monuments, with up to three massive ramparts. But they may not have been primarily for defence, for there are gaps in the fortifications. They are larger, and their pottery has curvilinear and stamped decoration. The ramparts are of earth and stone rubble, without the dry-stone walling. There is no evidence that these were ever attacked. Uley Bury is the finest example, and Brackenbury Ditches near Wotton-under-Edge and Kimsbury hill fort on Painswick Beacon also date from this time. The latter has been partly destroyed by quarrying.

During the Iron Age, the Cotswolds were grazed by cattle and sheep, and both wheat and barley were grown, so farming was mixed. Excavation has shown that the hill forts were lived in. However, their sites are very exposed, particularly when conditions are bleak in winter, and their lack of a nearby water supply would have been a handicap for long periods of occupancy. One assumes that most of the population lived on lower, more sheltered ground close to springs, and used the hill forts in times of war when invasion threatened. The famous Birdlip mirror and Bagendon brooches found on Barrow Wake in the late nineteenth century, and now in Gloucester Museum, display the sophisticated metalworking skills of this early period.

Hill forts are not the only prehistoric features along the Cotswold Way. Belas Knap is the most conspicuous Neolithic long barrow of the Cotswolds. Although it has been restored, the fine dry-stone walling of its false entrance and the stone chambers along its sides give a good impression of the typical form of these structures. The excavated contents of Belas Knap are in the Cheltenham Museum and also indicate a pastoral economy with some crop cultivation 4,000 years ago. But once again, we do not know exactly where the people lived. The Cotswold Way passes other long barrows at Shurdington and Nympsfield, and Hetty Peglers Tump is not far from its route. Long barrows are not confined to the Cotswold Edge, however, but are widely distributed over the dip slope as well.

The Cotswold Way also passes by a few Roman villa sites. Above the reservoirs at Great Witcombe the footings of a wealthy villa, with fragments of mosaic floors, have been uncovered. Roman villas were the centres of country estates producing wool and corn for sale in the urban markets. So road access was as important as suitable farmland. The Witcombe site is ideal for this purpose with its spring and Ermin Way leading to Gloucester. Villas were often in pairs and the complementary villa here was at Dryhill, just below Crickley Hill.

As we walk above the Witcombe villa we have entered a wooded section of the Cotswold Way. The mature beech woods of the Cotswold edge are variously managed by organisations such as Natural England, the National Trust, the Woodland Trust and Gloucestershire County Council, and some are privately owned. Typically these beech woods are located on the upper slopes of the escarpment and in some places as

Walking in mature beechwoods near Brockworth.

at Cranham they extend on to the eastern slopes as well. Some woods have been coppiced, but most beech trees are standards with impressively straight boles. There is some genetic variation among the trees, and in Brockworth Wood a number of trees have rather grotesque forms. The understorey is of hazel, holly and yew, and both ash and sycamore are intermingled with the mature beech trees. Dense summer shade, deep and slowly decomposing litter, and pathogens produced by the shallow rooting beech trees, limit the ground flora to relatively few species. But there are spectacular displays of wood anemones, bluebells and wild garlic in the spring and scattered clusters occur of spurge laurel, green and stinking hellebore, wood sanicle, nettle leaf bellflower, lesser periwinkle and herb Paris. The bird population includes woodpeckers, tits, tree creepers and buzzards, and roe deer and badgers are common. In winter the uneven ground surface of the woodland is better exposed, with frequent traces of quarrying, terracing and earthworks, as well as evidence of the natural processes of solifluction and slumping. But it is the bright spring green of the foliage and the rich autumnal tints that chiefly characterise these woods and attract the visitor.

Several woods warrant special attention from the walker. Lineover

Wood, south-east of Cheltenham is an ancient deciduous wood, distinguished, as its name indicates, by lime trees. 'Lineover' is derived from the Saxon for lime bank. In the upper part of the wood large-leafed lime trees are still growing, and one coppice stool is considered to be more than 1,000 years old. Other trees such as oak and ash have also been coppiced, and so too has the understorey of hazel, birch and maple. The wood is now managed by the Woodland Trust, and its glades provide habitats for butterflies including the silver-washed fritillary. The increasingly rare combination of lily-of-the-valley and angular Solomon's seal is found in the woodland flora here, as it is in several other scarp-face woods, and toothwort grows on the roots of hazel shrubs.

Once we cross the top of the escarpment west of Painswick, the Cotswold Way passes through more beech woods. Long ago C. Henry Warren, in his book *A Cotswold Year*, commented on the greenness of these woods. In summer, sunlight is filtered through the leaves of the beech trees and the sycamore saplings on to an understorey of holly and yew and to a ground flora of ivy, hart's tongue fern, moss and dog's mercury. Plants of spurge laurel are scattered through the wood, garlic and wood anemones cover large areas in spring, and there are many predominantly green flowering plants such as moschatel. Warren describes the woods 'as secretive from the outside, green within, even the air seems green'. It is only in winter, when the branches of the mature trees are bare and the ground is covered with dead leaves, that there is a change to browns and greys. Along the lower edges of the woods animals and birds have a more varied habitat, here badger sets are common and the scent of the fox frequently indicates its recent passage.

In all these woods we may notice that the preferred habitats of the spring flowers differ slightly. Primroses and violets grow best on banks which receive shafts of light, wood anemones flourish on better drained sites, and garlic spreads on damper areas. Brambles are often found under ash, and bluebells form a carpet under beech. Where old permanent pasture borders the woods, there is the tendency for scrub to spread on to the grassland. At one time thorn bushes covered large areas of the Cotswolds, and for the conservation of the flowers of the grassland it is necessary to check this scrub. The stocky and hardy Belted Galloway breed of cattle have been found ideal for this purpose, and they may be seen at various places along the Cotswold Way.

Despite the reference to 'charming villages' in the publicity flier advertising the Cotswold Way, there are no villages on the edge. The trail has to descend to the foot of the escarpment for villages, and this it does at Stanton. Stanton is one of the 'show piece' Cotswold villages. Soon after the Dissolution the land passed to a group of yeomen farmers, and their substantial farmhouses are major components of the village. Some have dates and initials inscribed on the stonework, including 'TW 1577' for Thomas Warren, one of those yeomen, on the house now called the Manor. Most of the village was bought in 1906 by Sir Philip Stott, and he began a programme of restoration of the properties which continued for the next twenty-five years or so, and the present-day appearance of the village owes much to his sympathetic handling. There is a village cross of medieval origin, with a seventeenth-century sun dial and globe and cross above. Its simplicity contrasts with the finely sculptured war-memorial cross in the churchyard, carved by Sir Ninian Comper, who also provided many modern architectural features for the church. His insignia, found in a lower corner of the church windows, is a wild strawberry flower. This church is well worth a visit. It has flagstone floors, and the benches beneath the gallery have poppy heads. The grooves in the woodwork here are where shepherds tied their dogs. There is a rare fourteenth-century wooden pulpit and the fifteenth-century glass in the east window came from Hailes Abbey. We may notice, too, the carved face of the sun high on the south wall of the nave. The ribbed spire and battlements are also attractive external features. As with other carefully restored villages, Stanton has its own design of street lanterns.

An interesting characteristic of the spring line villages of the north Cotswolds is their monastic connections. The sequence of manors along the escarpment had, until the Dissolution, different monastic owners. For Broadway ownership was by Pershore Abbey, for Buckland it was St Peter's Abbey in Gloucester, for Stanton it was Winchcombe Abbey and for Stanway it was Tewkesbury Abbey. Didbrook belonged to Hailes Abbey. It is not unusual to find adjacent manors formerly owned by monasteries, but it is unusual to have so many different monastic owners as we have here, and as is to be expected, we find marks of this varied ownership in the churches.

If there are few villages along the Cotswold Way, the deficiency is more than made up by the market towns visited. Chipping Campden, Broadway, Winchcombe, Painswick, Dursley and Wotton-under-Edge were all market towns. Apart from Winchcombe, which was an important town in Saxon times, their charters date from the twelfth and thirteenth centuries when they were planned towns, with burgage plots laid out beside the broad market street or marketplace. At Chipping Campden the Market Hall in the High Street, built for the sale of butter, cheese and poultry, was given by Sir Baptist Hicks in 1627 and bears his coat of arms. The Market House in Dursley is in the town centre and was built in 1738. It stands on Tuscan pillars, rather like those of Tetbury. In a niche on the east side is a statue of Queen Anne, who had died some twenty-four years earlier, and on the south side are the arms of the Estcourt family, who were lords of the manor and built the Market House. This building is very well maintained. Market towns usually had grammar schools. Chipping Campden's, founded by John Fereby, dates from the fifteenth century and Katherine Lady Berkeley's School at Wotton-under-Edge, founded in 1384, is one of the oldest in the country. Markets brought prosperity to these towns and this wealth, linked to that gained from the sale of wool and from the later woollen industry of the south Cotswolds, explains the high quality of their seventeenth- and eighteenth-century houses. The use of a common building material and traditional skills has made it possible for houses which are unique in design to blend together marvellously. Few streets can compare archi-

The Market House, Dursley with the figure of Queen Anne.

The magnificently carved stonework of the church tower, Chipping Campden.

tecturally with the High Street of Chipping Campden. The former clothiers' houses in Painswick and Wotton-under-Edge, Hugh Perry's Almshouses in Church Street, Wotton-under-Edge, which were built in 1638 around a grassed court and with their own chapel, and the woollen mills in the valley bottoms enhance the urban landscapes. And so do the great wool churches. The exterior of the three-staged west tower of Chipping Campden church with its pinnacles and wind vanes glinting in the sun and its decoration of delicately carved vertical ribs ending in ogee shaped moulds is the finest.

Winchcombe church is the simplest, and has a unity of construction in that it was completely rebuilt in the fifteenth century. It also has a three-staged west tower and its gilded weathercock catches the eye, as does the set of grotesque gargoyles which surrounds the building. The tower of Dursley church with its ornate parapet and pinnacles, also rises above the surrounding buildings, and on closer inspection is seen to be built not only of Cotswold limestone but also of local tufa.

The Cotswold Way passes several other notable landmark buildings. On the highest part of the north Cotswolds is Broadway Tower. Its plan is hexagonal, and at alternate angles, round towers rise to turrets. H.A .Evans compared it to the castle of a giant chess set. It is a folly, and was built in 1800 by James Wyatt for the Earl of Coventry, to be visible from the latter's residence at Croome Park near Worcester, where Wyatt was also working. It now houses a small exhibition giving details of its incidental history. William Morris and his family stayed in the tower for a holiday in 1876, and here he drafted notes which led to the formation of a society to protect ancient buildings from over zealous and fashionable restoration. He was particularly concerned about the removal of medieval wall plaster and old floor tiles from the interior of churches, which had already diminished the interest of many local ones, including that of Chipping Campden. Other pre-Raphaelites used it as a holiday home, and for a time it accommodated the printing press of Sir Thomas Phillipps, the great book collector, who lived nearby at Middle Hill. It is well known for its extensive views – but on sunny anticyclonic days the visitor may be disappointed by haze in the valley below.

Standing on Nibley Knoll, and visible for miles around, is the 111ft-high monument to William Tyndale. The stone tower, completed in 1866 at a cost of £1550, was designed by S.S. Teulon, who also designed two other distinguished buildings in the county, Huntley church and

Tortworth Court. Tyndale is thought to have been born in 1494, possibly in North Nibley, although the family home was Melksham Court at Stinchcombe, and he later became tutor to the family of Sir John Walsh at Little Sodbury Manor. He was an accomplished Greek and Hebrew scholar, to whom we owe the first printed English Bible. He followed Erasmus' desire, expressed in the preface to his Greek New Testament, 'I wish that the farm worker might sing parts of them at the plough, that the weaver might hum them at the shuttle, and that the traveller might beguile the weariness of the way by reciting them'. In translating the Bible into his mother tongue, Tyndale was using the vernacular of the Vale of Berkeley. Some of its phrases come from sixteenth-century Gloucestershire.

Any weariness from walking the Cotswold Way is partly alleviated by the fresh breezes that are experience all along the escarpment and more so by the views westward over the Vale of Evesham in the north and the Severn valley further south. Topographs point to places sixty miles away, which are visible in good light conditions. 'Stunning views' is an appropriate accolade for the Cotswold Way.

In order to qualify for National Trail status, the Cotswold Way has been improved recently in several respects. Oak posts, with the acorn

The topograph near Haresfield Beacon with its relief model of the Cotswold Edge.

symbol, now mark its route with sufficient frequency that a map is no longer necessary to follow the route, although its other information may be invaluable. New stiles and gates with easier catches are in place, and the surface of the path has been strengthened. For the latter, dolomite chippings have sometimes been used. This is a more durable stone than the Oolitic limestone readily available along the way, but much less pleasant to walk on, and ecologically inappropriate. The path has also been rerouted to avoid the more dangerous road crossings, although the large volume of traffic at the top of Crickley Hill remains a hazard. There are many convenient car parks and picnic places along the Way, and at several cottages and farms refreshments may be obtained in addition to those available at the inns.

So for 104 miles the rambler may enjoy this long distance path through an Area of Outstanding Natural Beauty. At times the Cotswold Way meets some of the other paths discussed in this book. Close to Prestbury it crosses the Parliamentarian army route, at Birdlip that of the Welsh drovers, near King's Stanley the towpath of the Stroudwater bow-hauliers and between Hailes and Winchcombe it actually follows the pilgrims' way. And although it has a modern designation and as we have seen is of great interest to the contemporary geologist, archaeologist, botanist and student of architecture, it generally follows a route walked by man for more than 4,000 years.

For further reading: Mark Richards *The Cotswold Way* Reardon Publishing 1995.

ELEVEN

The Footpath Network – A Case Study in the Windrush Valley

Until this final chapter we have been concerned with paths that have been used for specific purposes. Now we will look at the whole network of paths, tracks and lanes in a sample Cotswold valley. The valley of the upper Windrush has been chosen for this case study because of the wide variety of paths that have been developed in and around the villages of Temple Guiting, Guiting Power and Naunton. The area has examples of paths that were mainly used as through routes in medieval times, others that were formed to meet the local needs of the communities, and yet others that in the last year or two have been designed for observing wildlife. The villages, which are adjacent, have contrasting layouts and different landscape histories. They are popular with today's leisure walkers following the Gloucestershire, Windrush and Wardens' Ways.

The internal form or layout of a village is largely determined by the framework made by its public open spaces. These may sometimes include greens of various shapes and sizes as with Guiting Power, but always include roads, tracks and paths. This framework controls the arrangement of the building plots and within these the spacing of the houses. Until quite recently, most ordinary farm buildings and cottages only lasted for a century or two, but the building plots in the heart of a village have been much more durable. They are normally far older than the present day houses, although they too may have changed over time through amalgamation or division. The routeways are older still and have been the most constant elements in the village plan, often dating back by more than 800 years to an early plan. Some villages on the Cotswolds, which had Saxon origins, were replanned in or shortly after Norman times, and where their name includes that of a manorial family or a royal or ecclesiastical owner, this name may give a clue as to the authority responsible for the replanning. 'Temple' from the Knights' Templar and 'Power' are examples.

Most early users of the routeways travelled on foot. The distinction between main roads, lanes, bridleways and footpaths, that we find today, was not made then. For a pedestrian there was little difference between walking along an unmetalled road, such as a Cotswold white way, and walking along a bridle way or footpath. In fact, the footpath may have been preferred as it was less likely to be rutted and muddy in wet weather. And as the early routeways were of more or less equal importance to the villagers, so too was their influence on the village plan.

In contrast to the persistence of the routeways within the villages, those outside the built up area may have experienced major changes. This is mainly because of the re-organisation of the rural landscape through the eighteenth-century Parliamentary Enclosure Act. As a result of these Acts, the lands of the various landholders were reallocated, and the common open fields across which the villagers could walk freely were now subdivided into the hedged and walled fields we see today. From this time onwards many old paths were closed and walking was largely restricted to the delimited public rights of way, some of which

A typical Cotswold whiteway.

were completely new. In the study area the hedge beside a path may give supporting evidence for the path's age. As noted earlier, if it contains such shrubs as hazel, field maple, and dogwood, and trees of crab apple, ash and oak, species that would not have been deliberately planted to provide a stock proof boundary, it is likely to be an old hedge and the path beside it may also be old, predating the Parliamentary Enclosure Act of the parish.

In the case study we will first look briefly at each of the three villages in turn, considering their layouts and routeways. Reference to the OS Explorer Map OL45 'The Cotswolds' may be helpful in following the text. Although there is a marked clustering of houses around the church at the west end of Naunton, where several lanes originally converged on the ford and later on the bridge over the river Windrush, this is essentially a linear village, stretched out for a mile along its main street. The street keeps to the north side of the river and most houses are on the gravelly and more gently sloping south-facing side of the valley. This is a significant site factor in winter, when the low sun hardly rises above the steeper south side of the valley, and where the shadows can remain all day. The lanes coming into the main street from the north descend along dry valleys from the plateau above, and from the south west another lane descends diagonally across the steep valley side from the old Gloucester

A sunken way leading down to Naunton from the Gloucester to Stow-on-the-Wold road.

to Stow-on-the-Wold road. This latter road was turnpiked in 1755, but it is much older than this. Three footpaths also descend from this through road to crossing points of the river, giving access to different parts of the village. There is also a wider trackway from the village which crossed the turnpike road and continues south, now as a footpath, to the parish boundary and then on to the village of Notgrove. Its sunken nature as it climbs up from the river Windrush indicates long usage. It is the ancient pathway that separated the east side from the west side of Naunton's Upper End common field. It was the routeway both for livestock from the village, as they moved out to graze these fields when they were in fallow, and for the plough teams and harvest wagons, when the strips of these open fields were cultivated for corn. Its significance declined after the parish Enclosure Act of 1778, when scattered independent farms were formed and the village was no longer the main centre for farming activities. The equivalent routeway to the north of the village, giving access to Naunton's Lower End common field and separating its eastern part from its western, was the lane towards Summerhill.

Guiting Power is a nodal village centred on its two small greens. These form the hub of six radiating routeways. The road following the Windrush valley, which may have been a saltway at the time of the Domesday Book because both Guiting Power and Temple Guiting

The old trackway from Guiting Power church towards the mill on the river Windrush.

had salt connections with Droitwich, bypasses the village. But another important road, which linked the ancient Saxon town of Winchcombe with Stow-on-the-Wold, runs through it. Both Winchcombe and Stow were the early markets for these villages. Guiting Power, which is half way between them, received its own market charter in 1330 and we would expect it to have been a focus of early local routeways. The other lanes and tracks connect it to neighbouring settlements such as the villages of Hawling and Naunton, the hamlet of Barton, and the deserted medieval village of Castlett. Houses extend for a short way along each of these lanes. The church is at a distance from the village centre, but earthworks in the adjacent fields indicate that once there were more buildings near to it. Another shallow sunken way links it to the main road through the village and leads on to the former corn mill on the Windrush. A large segment of the parish to the west of the village has now no public rights of way. There are farm tracks to two isolated hill barns and probably these originally dated from the time of Guiting Power's Enclosure Award in 1798, when earlier paths here were closed.

Temple Guiting also has earthworks close to the church, indicating an earlier settlement on its south side. The fourteenth-century Manor Farm, on the north side, is the oldest surviving house in all three parishes. Temple Guiting is one of the largest Cotswold parishes and has four evenly spaced,

A clapper bridge over the river Windrush at Kineton.

small discrete settlements along the Windrush valley, namely Ford on the Tewkesbury to Stow-on-the-Wold road, which was turnpiked in 1792, Temple Guiting itself, Kineton and Barton. Each of the four settlements has a bridge or ford crossing the river. Pinnock, over the brow of the hill to the west, was another deserted medieval village, and is connected by an old track and a footpath to Temple Guiting. The Enclosure Award for the parish was made in 1805, when a large proportion of the land had been acquired by one principal land holder, George Talbot of Temple Guiting House, and the pattern of older trackways now influenced the reallocation of land to the other landholders. The procedure for this land redistribution at the time of enclosure will be considered later, but we may note here that not only have these early paths affected the layout of villages, they may also account for some of the more unusual patterns of the land holdings.

When villages were largely self supporting and only relied on market towns for the few goods they could not obtain from within their own territory, a portion of land was allocated to supply each of the basic requirements. Thus there was a large area of land in arable use for growing corn, meadow land beside the river was for cattle and hay crops, pasture land on the higher ground was for sheep. There was also woodland for fuel and timber and in many cases the village exploited a quarry for building stone. For these various resources paths were set out to allow the villagers easy access. If it was a point resource like a quarry or a spring the paths were fixed. For arable land, meadows and woods, movement was less curtailed, though there were commonly used tracks. Self supporting villages were in existence as early as Saxon times and the three villages considered in this study, together with the additional manors of Pinnock, Castlett, Aylworth and Harford now within their parishes, are all recorded in the Domesday Book. So it is likely that all such access paths were in existence before 1086, the date of the book's survey.

In the upper part of the Windrush valley common arable fields were on the land above the steeply incised valley bottoms. The soil here is thin and brashy and grain yields would have been relatively low. To maintain fertility the fields were cultivated in alternate years with the land left fallow in the other years. Cotswold settlements were therefore generally characterised by a two-field system of farming. Each of the nucleated settlements had trackways leading to these fields, which are preserved in today's landscape. They are wider than footpaths, often sunken, as we have seen in the case of Naunton, and may zig-zag where the gradient is steep, as is well illustrated at Barton. The dry grassland on the hills was the most suitable land for sheep grazing, and the same tracks used for arable farming would have been used to move sheep back to the village farmsteads when a more sheltered environment was required in winter or at lambing time. The valley floors of the Windrush and its tributaries are narrow and, apart from the Swillies near Lower Harford, meadow land was scarce. Therefore cattle were also kept on the higher ground, and Isaac Taylor's map of 1777 indicates that the hills east of the Windrush valley were used for cow pastures.

Until its replanting in the mid-twentieth century, Guiting Wood was an outstanding example of a medieval wood. The *Domesday Book* records woodland at Temple Guiting and this wood retains many typical signs of an ancient wood. Its irregular, banked outline, followed in places by parish boundary lines; its interior divisions, formerly associated with coppicing; its ground flora which still includes lily of the valley and wood anemones, are all diagnostic features. Holloways lead from the wood, and along them timber and fuel would have been carried. Both Temple Guiting and Guiting Power probably used this resource and another source of fuel for the villagers was gorse. The Enclosure Award for Temple Guiting refers to Poors' Furze, an area east of the village, from which gorse could be cut and carried along the track which passes Wells Head. Some gorse remains today in Gorse Valley near Barton and on one or two other steep slopes, but most has been cleared. Naunton was less well provided with timber, though there was an extensive wood on Grange Hill close to the parish boundary.

Nine watermills were recorded in the three parishes in 1086, an indication of the significance of corn growing in the area and also of the availability of waterpower. In fact, the place name 'Guiting' means a torrent. Two of these mills at Barton had become fulling mills by the end of the twelfth century, when we have the first documentary reference to cloth production on the Cotswolds. Corn mills imply access routes for farm wagons, and no doubt some of the tracks crossing the Windrush and its main tributary through Castlett and Pinnock were made for this purpose.

The Oolitic limestone of the area has been quarried for building stone from the time when stone replaced timber as the principal building material. Old quarries are widespread, but there were two very important quarrying areas here, one was for Guiting stone, a honey-coloured building stone, and the other for Stonesfield slate, the traditional Cotswold roofing stone. Not only were some quarrymen employed all year round, but winter employment in these quarries was also found for farm workers as stone was extracted and slates were shaped by hand. Some Oxford colleges used stone from Naunton and the control of the quarries at Chalk Hill, on the east of the area, was retained by Corpus Christi College at the time of Enclosure. Road and river transport was used for this exported stone, but the roads would have been those already in existence rather than newly made. Paths from the villages to the quarries were used by the workmen.

The Domesday Book mentions priests at both Guiting Power and Temple Guiting and the churches here and at Naunton have Norman architectural features in their fabric. There was also a church at Pinnock and probably one at Aylworth, where the field name 'Lady's Hays' may indicate its site. Hays means an enclosure and Lady refers to St Mary. As the settlements were essentially nucleated, there was not the need for the numerous paths to church from isolated houses that we find in some other areas. However, fourteenth-century settlement reorganisation and some desertion at the time of the Black Death would have meant a

The earthworks of the Lower Harford deserted medieval village are beyond the farm buildings.

degree of population movement, and the few people that remained to work the land at the deserted sites would have needed paths or tracks to link them with the main settlements for church and for other social and economic provisions.

The small enclosures near the villages are generally old, but most land in the three parishes was open until the Parliamentary Enclosure Acts. Following the Enclosure Award, the new farm boundaries were carefully marked out on the ground for the commissioners, who were responsible for the land reallocation. Walls had to be built or hedges planted along these farm boundaries within the first year. Then the interior divisions of the farm into its required number of fields could take place at the discretion of the land holder. Gates and stiles were erected in the field boundaries so that, while pedestrians could cross the land, farm live-stock could not freely move from field to field. The Enclosure Awards also specified the widths of the public rights of way across the land. The commissioners were required to act fairly and impartially on behalf of all landholders. This implied not only fairness in the area of land each person received, but also in the quality of land and with respect to the distance from their farmstead. An interesting example of the application of impartiality occurs at Kineton. There were six relatively small land-

The trackway to the blocks of land held by Kineton farmers. Each land unit had its own barn.

holders here in 1805, and each was granted some land adjacent to their home. But for the remainder of their land holding, another strip of land was granted to each farmer on the higher ground to the east. Each of the parallel plots of land here had a barn from which the more distant farming operations could take place. In this way land area, land quality and distance were equitably distributed. To link the farmsteads in Kineton to the more distant plots, the lane and track towards Lots barn was used. This routeway undoubtedly influenced the commissioners in the location of the new holdings. There may be more to it than this, however, because some of the enclosures on the high ground are referred to as 'ancient enclosures' and are therefore older than the Enclosure Award. Perhaps the Kineton farmers already had some enclosed land on the higher ground. When a landholder possessed freehold land, this was also considered by the commissioners, and frequently new land was granted beside this. Such was the case with the two large farms at Barton. Another change associated with enclosure was the commuting of tithes. Formerly, a tithe of the agricultural produce of each farm was passed to the church. When tithes were commuted, an area of land equivalent to the tithe was granted to the church. As this was an entirely new and a large element in land holding, it was common for the church land to be on the edge of the parish. At Temple Guiting the church land became Trafalgar Farm, which is in the extreme north east of the parish, and so named after the contemporary battle.

In this way the pattern of roads, tracks and paths of these three parishes has evolved. Most components were for local use, but some were in a sense imposed from outside. The development of the turnpike roads is the main example of this, but there were others. A parish boundary in the north west follows Campden Lane. This lane was a medieval routeway used for the transport of wool by packhorse from Chipping Campden to the exporting port of Southampton. Another early through route was Buckle Street, which follows the ridge on the east of the area and makes part of Naunton's parish boundary. This road is also at least medieval in origin, and it may be much older because it connects with the Roman Fosse Way near Bourton Bridge. The pack horse transport of salt would have also necessitated a through route.

Writers on the Cotswolds at the end of the nineteenth century frequently mention the attractive walks in this area. Walkers then seem not to have been constrained to following the public rights of way. They wandered across the fields, and farmers did not object. After the First World War attitudes changed, notices that 'trespassers will be prosecuted' appeared, and leisure walking could only follow the footpaths, and frequently this was with some difficulty. Barbed wire and other blockages presented obstacles to walkers, and ramblers were clearly unwelcome. This is how Algernon Gissing describes the situation in the early twentieth century in his *The Footpath Way in Gloucestershire*:

> In the old days the word 'trespassing' never entered one's mind in wandering about these uplands. So long as you left gates closed or open as you found them, did not damage a wall or fence in getting over it, and otherwise behaved as a well-conditioned mortal, your presence, by farmer, keeper, or shepherd, seemed to be welcomed rather than otherwise. Many a delightful interchange of experience was naturally the result. But a different spirit seems to be creeping over the land now. Barbed wire is coming more and more into fashion; actual pathways are being blocked up; stiles are being made as far as possible insurmountable.

He attributed this unfortunate development to the change in land ownership, as the large estates were broken and sold off. The new owners did not have the same outlook as the former landed gentry, and he regretted the latter's passing. Today, conditions for leisure walkers are much improved. Paths are generally well cared for, stiles are regularly maintained and waymarking is clear. It is easy to follow the long distance footpaths that cross the area. The Windrush Way and the Wardens' Way are popular routes, and following recent legislation and a new approach to conservation grants to farmers, fresh areas of land are becoming accessible to walkers. Permissive paths and open access land have created new opportunities for experiencing the countryside, and they occur in our area as in others. One of the most informative is a new wildlife walk at Bemborough Farm, beside the Cotswold Farm Park. It includes both breezy high wold and sheltered valley sides in its two-mile trail. The walk has been designed to display the methods and benefits of environmentally friendly farming, and at the same time give the public access to old pastureland, which has never received chemical applications in the form of inorganic fertilizers or sprays. The focus is on encouraging biodiversity in an area of limestone grassland. The trail passes through Barton Larches, now a site of special scientific interest (SSSI). This is a

An information board on the wildlife walk at the Cotswold Farm Park.

site where shallow quarrying for roof slates once took place and scrub subsequently spread over the stoney waste. But in the thin stoney soil, where many high-nutrient demanding plants cannot survive, more delicate and increasingly rare species can flourish. It is one of the few places where in some years the rare Cotswold pennycress may be seen in numbers, and the more conspicuous meadow saxifrage. The information boards on the walk are outstanding in their coverage of the plants, insects, birds and mammals in each habitat and of the old man-made features to be seen. Several farms in the Windrush valley have a nature conservation policy, and there is also a scattering of other fields to which there is open access under the recent Countryside Stewardship Scheme, but this is the first to be clearly and effectively displayed to the public. It also incorporates part of the old trackway which gave access to the more distant plots of land of the Barton farms at the time of the Parliamentary Enclosure Acts.

Although one footpath through the fields may seem to be like any other, they may have had very different histories, as this case study demonstrates. And to walk them with an understanding of their histories and of the people for whom they were originally designed surely enhances the experience.

For further reading: Alan Pilbeam *The Landscape of Gloucestershire*

Tempus 2006.

Index of Gloucestershire Places

If you are interested in purchasing other books published by The History Press
or in case you have difficulty finding any of our books in your local bookshop,
you can also place orders directly through our website

www.thehistorypress.co.uk